MINERS 1984–1994

MINERS

1984–1994

A Decade of Endurance

Edited by

Joe Owens

Living Memory

Polygon

First published by Polygon
22 George Square
Edinburgh

Set in Weiss
by ROM-Data Corporation Ltd, Falmouth, Cornwall
Printed and bound in Great Britain by
Short Run Press Ltd, Exeter

A CIP record for this book is available from the British Library

ISBN 0 7486 6162 X

CONTENTS

THE MINERS' WELFARE

Bathgate Road, Blackburn.

On the road up from the Cross
is the ground where the Miners' stood,
a blasted site, strewn with rubble.
One can pan back through time,
like an archaeological excavation
and observe that, before the Club
was built and razed,
this was the miners' quoiting-green,
levelled for the purpose
by teams of men on summer evenings.

One summer morning in childhood,
in a leafy lane I was startled by men
exotic as blackamoors
with lights in their heads,
returning home while a new coffle toiled,
pale as ghosts, in the labyrinths below.

At week-ends, the Miners' detonated into life,
with dancing, drinking and fighting.
There are no miners around here now;
they've been summoned up from darkness
into a world of light.
Where giant wheels pitched against the sky
and where heavy wagons clashed,
all is now sealed and silent as graves.
From these pits there is no resurrection.

Dennis O'Donnell

INTRODUCTION

In 1946, the French writer Albert Camus defined the experience of the Spanish Civil War in the 1930s as one through which men learned that '. . . one can be right and yet be beaten, that force can defeat spirit, that there are times when courage is not its own reward.'

Ten years ago a kind of civil war was fought in the British coalfields when, in 1984, two forces faced up to one another and began a year long campaign that signalled both an end and a beginning for both of them. The miners' strike of 1984–85 remains the most bitterly contested industrial dispute in twentieth-century British labour history. Its denouement, like that of Camus's Spain, taught the men and women who fought it a series of cruel lessons about justice and retribution, power against will and the consequences of perfidy and defeat.

Events that year challenged not only those directly affected by the strike but society as a whole to re-examine old certainties. It exposed the threads of mythology and ideology that interweave to form a blanket impression of a society with systemised values about right and wrong, common purpose and a shared sense of identity to the fire test of confrontation between the representatives of two classes; fundamentally opposed economic interests faced each other across an ideological chasm.

Part of the Scargill myth (ironically enriched by his overnight mutation from the Big Bad Wolf to Little Red Riding Hood during the coal debacle of 1992-93) concludes that had someone else been the miners' leader in 1984 the strike would have been brought to an 'honourable conclusion' at least six months earlier than it was. It encapsulates the absurdity that one man kept, against their will and the best attempts of everyone else involved, 100,000 miners and their families out on strike for the best part of a year.

This theory misses the point. Quite apart from the dubious psychology of a Tory Government bent on revenge for defeats in the 1970s on one side and a manipulating, bug-eyed revolutionary on the other, all the evidence confirms that the strike had been planned years in advance by the Tories. It was to be a setpiece confrontation. First mooted in the now infamous Ridley Report published in the *Economist* while they were still in opposition, the Tories implemented the practical preparatory steps vital to any battle with the miners early into their administration.

Coal stocks were built up from 37.7 million tonnes in 1980 to 58 million by 1983. Private, non-unionised, road haulage companies, like Yuill and Dodds in Scotland, were increasingly introduced to transport coal with the aim of neutralising any potential solidarity action from transport workers.

Power stations were switched to dual coal/oil burning. In 1981, the Central Electricity Generating Board (CEGB) was asked to prepare a contingency plan for a miner's strike by Sir Donald Maitland, the Energy Permanent Secretary – it was ready within months. That same year, the Tories backed away from a confrontation with the NUM calculating that they were not yet ready for it. In the meantime, trade union legislation made its way through parliament, as it has done ever since, and the notorious Ian McGregor was appointed chairman of the Coal Board.

I have listed those measures, not as part of a history of the strike – that is not the intention of this introduction – but to illustrate the degree of preparation undertaken by the government prior to March 1984. This was to be no ordinary industrial dispute. The real point of the confrontation was political: to begin the emasculation of the trade union and labour movement and remove it as a force from society.

The place of the NUM within British society has never been seriously questioned. Even at its numerically weakest, at the time of the Heseltine announcement that 30,000 jobs were to go in October 1992, it was capable of inspiring the sympathy of millions and a march of hundreds of thousands.

The miners were as beloved by the most notoriously sentimental in the labour movement as they were hated by the bowler hats in the City and the pinstriped zealots in the Cabinet. Taking them on was a quite simple calculation: defeat and humiliate the trade union movement's 'Brigade of Guards' and the rest will lie down and play dead.

It was an audacious gamble by a government driven to take it, the odds heavily stacked in its favour, by the economic imperatives they had embraced. These were indeed to be New Times, but not the kind envisaged by the political toddlers from the end of history, death of socialism, birth of the post-modern illusion kindergarten. These times would come to be characterised by the 'management's right to manage'; telephone digit salaries for the chairmen of privatised natural resources and the abolition of wages councils; the return of mass unemployment and the emergence of Guinness as a cure for dementia; the marketing of UK plc as the home of low wages and the strictest anti-trade union legislation outside Turkey; and the slight but unmistakable stench of a re-emergent fascism.

Gambles taken on the economic front throughout the Lawson boom (the same Nigel who memorably remarked while Energy Minister in 1984 that public money spent defeating the miners was 'a worthwhile investment for the good of the nation') were going to leave behind bills that had to be paid. The only question was about who was going to settle them.

Cowing the trade unions and setting the agenda for the Labour Party would mean that burden could be shifted onto the shoulders of working people. And so it came to pass. But how?

As I said earlier, this introduction is not a chronological history of that year's events. It is written by someone who, aged nineteen, went on strike for the first time in 1984 and for whom the experience has left an indelible ensemble of memories and lasting impressions. It left, as Gramsci described 'knowing thyself', an infinity of traces without leaving an inventory. For me, like thousands of others, it was an extraordinary experience which continues to exercise a significant influence over my political and cultural growth in myriad ways, conscious and unconscious, good and bad.

Without qualification, it has constituted so far the single most important and formative experience in my life, the birth of my son notwithstanding. I resent nothing about it, though I do have regrets. I feel privileged to have fought it. I wept when it ended and on the day three years later when they shoved us out on the stones with shitpence compensation; and I wept again in 1992 when another 30,000 men and their families faced what men I knew had faced. Everything to do with the experience is still raw and ten years later the rage is still with me. I think it always will be.

This introduction will be a personal account and analysis of why the miners were defeated then and where we are now. Not only we, the miners, but the movement to which we belonged and which still claims, with increasingly less credibility, to represent our interests. As I write, the 1993 Labour Party Conference is taking place but the television is switched off because I want time for sober reflection and cannot afford the exasperation its mediocrity and political illiteracy inflict on me. Suddenly I remember lobbying a Labour Party gathering years ago and shouting to the late John Smith as he went in (I cannot remember what position he held then) that socialism was spelled 'S-O-C-I-A-L-I-S-M'. I called out the letters one by one. He turned back and said 'That's not funny.' He was right.

In his work, *The Eighteenth Brumaire of Louis Bonaparte*, Marx writes that although men make their own history, they do not make it as they please or under circumstances of their choosing. Since 1984, many people have written about the miners' strike from a range of perspectives. Some see glory where others find parody. Some take from its spirit optimism for the future where others, again, see only ghosts from an irretrievable past. Its significance is rarely, however, questioned.

The dispute blasted onto the scene barely six months after it had become a commonplace in the labour movement that the days of strikes and picket lines had faded away like old banners. There was a 'new working class' who voted Tory. It was time to jettison old beliefs and adapt to the need for change. The old traditions had to be replaced with new ideas, these were New Times which demanded a New Reality and new clichés. In the wake of a second Thatcher victory, this was code for wholesale defeatism, abject surrender.

Yet just as these intellectual colossi finished dancing an entrechat in celebration of their most recent pretext for institutionalised inertia, the coalfields erupted in precisely the fashion they had judged historically redundant. Unfortunately, there were other traditions that had managed to survive the composite resolutions of the conference halls, in particular, that old trouper: the sell-out.

With a few honourable exceptions, the trade union leaders never matched the flatulence of their rhetoric with concrete solidarity action. Despite their attempts to 'give an appearance of solidity to pure wind' as Orwell would have it, any excuse, from the lack of a ballot to the impossibility of convincing their members and from picket line violence to the price of mince, was conscripted to justify leaving the miners isolated against the might of a state machine and treasury ready to go to any length and expense to defeat them.

Let us examine one of those issues in more detail: the absence of a ballot. I single out this particular one because it haunted the NUM throughout that year and haunts it still. It provided an excuse for some and a rod for others and the miners were spared neither for those twelve months.

Very early on in the strike, the ballot ceased to become merely a mechanism, among others, available to the union through the rule book to consult its members on issues like industrial action. It rapidly began to exercise a talismanic effect on Tory ministers, the organised return to work movement (presently the UDM) and the right wing of the Labour Party and the trade unions.

The question of whether or not to have a ballot was deliberately and dishonestly elevated to the level of principle, when it should have remained where it belonged, as a matter of tactics. Crucially, the debate began to centre around the legitimacy of the strike without one. Chief among the most bitter opponents of the NUM who hung his hat on this particular peg was ex-UCS leader Jimmy Reid, whose columns in the *Daily Record* at the time, are so foam-specked in their venomous denunciations of Scargill and the strike that it is reasonable to assume that, had he been a miner in 1984, he would have been a scab. Like many ex-communists before him, his credentials as a heretic were finally supplanted by those of a renegade.

Within the rule book of the NUM, specifically Rule 41, the strike was perfectly constitutional. Two areas, Scotland and Yorkshire, called for action under their own rules and the union's National Executive declared it official. In time-honoured, and democratic tradition, picketing began and the strike spread according to the principle of the domino effect.

Yet, tactically, there should have been a ballot. It was a catastrophic mistake not to call one, particularly after a special conference in April 1984 had reduced the majority required from 55% to 50% plus one. No one seriously doubts a majority would have voted to continue the strike; we were already dug in by that time.

It would have won the Nottinghamshire miners over before a combination of time and resentment made that hope impossible. The impetus would have swung back to the NUM, its critics disarmed.

It did not happen. In the strike centres, we subscribed wholeheartedly to the idea that a man working in a coalfield safe from the threat of unemployment should not be allowed to vote another man out of his job. But the absence of that ballot did not, for us, remove one shred of legitimacy from our action. It was right to be on strike and the main task was to strengthen the forces already marshalled on the ground. By the end of April, the question had become academic to the vast majority of those miners on strike, who constituted the vast majority in the coalfield, yet it was an opportunity lost and it cost the union dearly, financially and morally, for the rest of the year.

The calendar year of the strike and the title of George Orwell's dystopia bore more in common than even he, in his wildest dreams of prophecy, could have hoped for; or feared. In Orwell's *1984* the writer portrayed the horror of life in a totalitarian state where Big Brother, the state, pervaded every aspect of life and in the image of a boot stamping on a human face for ever, provided one of the most haunting and enduring symbols of repression in world literature.

In Tory Britain in 1984, the experience of the miners' strike provided a contemporary glimpse of the immense power and potential brutality of the existing state machinery when it is swung into service on behalf of power.

The union was infiltrated and attempts made to destabilise it financially and organisationally. The apparat of the judiciary and the legislature assiduously pursued every legal avenue, however obscure, to find mechanisms to break the union. Basic civil rights of assembly, freedom of movement and freedom from arbitrary arrest were curtailed, even suspended. The right to work, seemingly inapplicable in the argument against pit closures and redundancies, was upheld with all the rigour and vigour of the law if it meant another man through the picket line.

For the police and their highly-trained, well-equipped and sophisticated riot squads, breaking the union had a more prosaic quality. The image of the thin blue line was replaced with that of the beefy paramilitary with the thick black truncheon and riot shield. Illusions of the police as just another emergency service were literally beaten out of miners and their families in scenes of quite sickening brutality. It was a lesson soon to be learned by people as diverse as the hippies at Stonehenge and the youth of Tottenham, the print workers at Wapping and, more recently, the poll-tax demonstrators in Trafalgar Square.

The most enduring legacy of the strike remains its mark on the lives and consciousness of the miners and their families. It was remarkable how fresh, sometimes raw, the memories were for all of us. For some of the interviewees, sitting down and reliving that year was a powerful and emotional experience. A decade later, tears are still shed openly when particularly personal or painful episodes flood back into the mind with all their tingling intensity undiminished by time. Some of the memories are, admittedly, sentimental; but others are bitter and sore and unhealed.

Nineteen eighty four is Year Zero – it is difficult to recall life before it. Life after the strike is different from before, despite the similarities; however far back from the centre stage to the wings we have travelled since then, the roars of approbation and the clamour of invective still ring in the ears. Some of the costumes have changed, but the plot remains the same, only now we understand it much better than we did before.

Life is not so much a matter of what American nineteenth-century writer Henry David Thoreau described as 'quiet desperation', it is more the anaesthetic of routine. Tragedy and comedy are played out in the home, the street and the pub; heroism is everyday life.

For thousands of men and women in the coalfields, the strike changed all that. The enormous centrifugal forces unleashed by the new challenges they faced threw them out of themselves and out into a world of new possibilities. For the women in particular, it was a revolution.

Life was no longer mainly about the house and the family, tea on the table and the washing machine. Opportunities to speak publicly, deal with the media, organise support groups – a gamut of activities – became the norm. The chaos and fragmentation that naturally sprung from being blasted out of life's continuum unleashed talents and confidence previously considered the preserve of others. Unrealised potential was discovered, aspirations grew with new horizons, the flowering was, as Dashiell Hammet writes in *The Maltese Falcon* 'like a fist when you open you hand'.

The tragedy is that when the strike ended, in the way that it did, the momentum was lost and the seemingly inescapable realities of pulling things back together again crowded in, leaving no room for most to nurture the seeds of ambition planted in them throughout the year. It was predictable, even inevitable, that that would happen, but no one went back under the anaesthetic, even though the return of certain elements of a previous routine was largely inescapable. The awakening had been too abrupt and the confrontation with issues previously unconsidered, too violent to be forgotten.

The decade since the strike has been calamitous for deep mining in Scotland. From fourteen pits in 1984 employing around 14,000 men, there are now two: Castlebridge in Fife and Monktonhall in Midlothian. The Frances colliery in Fife remains mothballed, on a care and maintenance basis. There are less than 2,000 people employed in the industry, once a powerhouse of local and national economies. The effects on support industries and the people employed in them have been no less catastrophic.

Following the 1992 announcement by the government of a further thirty-one pit closures nationally, economist Andrew Glyn of Corpus Christi College, Oxford, looked at the potential economic consequences of this wholesale shutdown. The loss of jobs, he predicted, could total in excess of 80,000. The increased unemployment would increase the government's deficit by some £1.2 billion in the first year (when redundancy payments would be made) and £0.5 billion thereafter as tax revenues were lost and benefits paid out. Everyone would then feel the inevitable repercussions: increased taxation or further cuts in public spending (leading to more unemployment) – or both. As I write, those jobs are already gone.

The Scottish experience since 1985 bears these conclusions out all too comprehensively. In Ayrshire in 1980 there were 3,821 people employed directly in the coal industry and four deep mines. By 1984, only two pits remained, Barony and Killoch, with 2,024 employees.

Ten years later, there is no deep mining in that coalfield and the last major employer to support the industry, J.H. Fenner, which made conveyor belts, closed in 1990 with the loss of 159 jobs.

The whole community has suffered as a result of the destruction of an industry that played a vital part in the local Cumnock and Doon Valley economy. By 1992, unemployment stood at 14.1%, well above both the Strathclyde and Scottish averages. A clearer indication of the human tragedy involved can be found in the figures relating to the duration of unemployment in the area.

In the New Cumnock and Catrine/Sorn/North Auchinleck wards, traditionally made up of miners and their families, 45.7% and

48.6%, respectively, of those out of work have been on the dole for more than a year – a direct consequence of the closedown of a major employer without any alternative jobs being created. It is illuminating to ponder, among all the others, the statistic that one in every three square metres of factory floorspace in that district is vacant. The defining feature of investment is its back, as it walks away.

Last year, I visited one of those areas to arrange to interview various ex-miners and include their observations in this book. Those interviews illustrate more eloquently than I can the toll that has been extracted from those people over the last ten years. But, even in the brief time I spent there, the sense of drift and emptiness was palpable in the lives of men and women whose talents and potential are being utterly squandered every day.

The focus that was provided by work, and the particular quality of community that sprung from the realities of working in the unique conditions of a pit, exist now only in shadows and shades. Every day is the same and the minutiae and gossip of those days, which before would have inhabited only the suburbs of people's consciousnesses, now play central roles. Life revolves around essentials with little opportunity to break out and away. Having travelled throughout the coalfield speaking to many different people, I discovered that these are common features of life after coal; after work has gone.

Of course it is not all bitterness and grey days. The resilience, humour and generosity of these communities is as genuine as it is astonishing. Individually, some people have been hit hard, but collectively, there is still a common spirit, however fractured, however fragile.

Yet our mining communities are still best defined by the paradox that there is so much in them lacking, that if they lacked one thing more, there would be no room for it.

Fear of that emptiness and insecurity were among the forces that drove men to involve themselves in setting up the Monktonhall

Miners' Cooperative. Whatever inherent flaws there were in the scheme, it was nevertheless a bold and ambitious challenge to the sense of inevitability that accompanied the pit closure programme.

The eventual collapse of the consortium into the hands of a private mining contractor cannot take away from the achievement of those miners in securing the future of that pit. But it was secured at a tremendous cost.

The history of that particular episode deserves to be examined in some detail and there is no space here to give it justice. I have no doubt, though, that the men and their families are entitled to an explanation from the their so-called financial and business advisers as to why they were allowed to twist in the wind for so long without the assistance that would have obviated the need to relinquish control and money to a private company. The Scottish Labour movement, which was remarkably muted considering its interests in mining elsewhere, also has a case to answer for leaving working people, struggling to maintain a grip on their livelihoods, isolated.

The mining communities are, however, not unique. Scotland as a whole has become an industrial necropolis as, one after another, factories and shipyards have closed down and their workers pushed out into an ever contracting jobs market. Gap sites where there were once workplaces have become symbolic of a different kind of emptiness imposed on people's lives.

And while that has being going on, in Britain as a whole, the gap between rich and poor keeps on growing. The Labour-sponsored Commission on Social Justice measured the number of people living in poverty as having risen to 11.3 million since 1979. The income of the poorest 10% fell by 14% while that of the top 10% rose by over half. One aspect of the human cost can be found in the fact that in Scotland, in Glasgow alone, the single most important factor in the death of young people has been revealed as fatal drug overdoses.

But what of the Labour movement while all of this has been going on? What leadership has been given, what opposition shown, what rage expressed in the face of the endless attacks on living standards and jobs and benefits across the whole spectrum of society since the Tories were first elected all those years ago? What indeed.

Following the defeat of the miners in 1985, the same people who had watched the strike go down to defeat without lifting a finger to help, now danced on its grave. The result of the strike gave the New Realists their second, slightly more rancid, wind. Once again, their glossy publications trumpeted the euphemisms and anti-theories of 'Post-Fordism' and 'New Times'. The perennial pessimists and cynics gathered around magazines like *Living Marxism* poured sneering scorn on 'narrow' perspectives like industrial action in favour of 'broad democratic alliances', flavoured condoms and boxer shorts embroidered with the word (surely passé) Proletariat.

It was a politics diluted and disfigured, a question of lifestyle choices rather than that of power, of no more historical consequence than the label on your shirt or the quality of this year's Beaujolais Nouveau. It was essentially the difference between those whose ignorance of the Marxism they deceitfully claimed their own condemned them to be perpetually confounded by events and those for whom events confirmed perspectives. Unfashionable language I know, but at least it is real.

Scargill, had by this time, of course, ceased to be the hero and had reverted in their eyes to type. The issue of leadership and its role in the labour movement became distorted through the prisms of personality and character (assassination).

The all too apparent flaws in the make-up of the NUM leader came to embody both the question and answer to the strike's defeat, conveniently diverting attention away from the responsibility carried by those whose lack of enthusiasm for a victory was only matched by the malevolence of their subsequent abuse.

Nowhere were these 'politics' more enthusiastically embraced than in the ranks of the Scottish Trade Union Congress (STUC) and Scottish NUM leaderships. In the case of the former, every time a factory or workplace, from Caterpillar through to Ravenscraig and Timex, was threatened with closure, the call went up for a 'broad alliance of the Scottish people' or some such trite phrase, to come together and save it, usually 'for the good of the nation as a whole'.

Not one single factory has remained open, not one single job saved. On every occasion, the same language was used and the same strategy employed and on every occasion it failed, miserably.

In place of 'narrow' perspectives they have substituted a preposterous political syncretism, characterised by ludicrously ineffective 'initiatives' like the Scottish Constitutional Convention. This retreat away from the 'traditional values' of the movement towards the loose aims and organisation of a pressure group has contributed nothing to the lives of those people seeing out their time on the dole in mining villages in Ayrshire and the steel towns of Lanarkshire. That, tragically, is the reality.

As for the Scottish NUM, they added to their neophytic enthusiasm for 'post-fordism' and all its attendant absurdities, a pathological hatred for All Things Scargill that would embarrass a member of the Conservative No Turning Back Group. Its political complexion is the same pastel shade as that of the STUC and the corollary has been the same: no broad, democratic wide-ranging alliance of the Scottish People or permutation thereof has saved a single mining job in Scotland since 1985.

Yet even that could have been explained away by dredging up other factors like the recession or the general political mood and attempting to put a spin on them that retained at least a veneer of credibility, were it not for the stance they took on the re-privatisation of the coal industry.

At the time of writing, the government has announced that its 'ultimate privatisation' would take the shape of selling British Coal assets in the form of five regional businesses, including Scotland.

No sooner had the minister in charge got the words out of his mouth than we were treated to a press conference announcing the setting up of Mining (Scotland) Ltd, eager to bid for its share of the spoils.

But it was to become more interesting yet. This venture, this universally condemned step among those who value life and limb above profit and loss, had the support of none other than the STUC and the Scottish mining trade unions. Led by a prominent Scottish Tory lawyer, Ross Harper, and the man responsible for fronting the closure of the Scottish coalfield in the late 1980s, George McAlpine, it came to prove that no alliance could be too broad.

From the unions we heard that they were opposed to privatisation 'in principle', a consideration that did not seem to trouble them unnecessarily while backing it in practice. So this was where the strategy of broad alliances led: to a place where principles are expendable, to the winner the spoils and to the same, our allegiance (for a share). This was the new reality: collaboration with a new generation of coal owners.

Whatever the depth of cynicism involved in that and other stunts, it should have come as little surprise. The British labour movement has become steadily more interested in the cut of its suit than the cut of its gib as one election humiliation has followed another. Policy has been dictated from the editorial conferences of the *Times* and the *Daily Mail*. No journey is too treacherous, providing it moves the party further to the right. Ideas, even terminology, involving anything resembling socialism are dubbed 'unfashionable' by the political couturier and ten years after Kinnock made the party 'electable', it remains in opposition.

To face the 'challenges of the future', a throwback to the Gaitskellite right wing in the shape of John Smith was elected leader. Strangely, his admission that he had not had a new idea in the forty years since he was a student did not pose a problem for a party whose political and 'intellectual' somersaults in the last ten years alone make Romanian gymnasts look lazy. Since his death, ironically, the prospect of Labour becoming a *genuine* alternative to the prevailing political logjam looks even more bleak.

Labour in the last decade resembles the fabled beaver, which, pursued by trappers who want its testicles from which medicinal drugs can be made, tears them off itself to save its life. What we are left with is politics without ideas or influence, passion or panache, power or responsibility.

This book is about one section of the working class, the miners and their families, who set an agenda in 1984–85 over which they had no control. Its aim is to provide a platform for them to describe their experiences, as individuals within their communities, since the end of a strike which they fought with the commitment and dignity that characterises them.

In the introduction to his book *The Age of Empire*, E.J. Hobsbawn argues that everyone is a historian in their consciously lived lifetime in as much as we come to terms with it in the mind, unreliable though that memory may be. The age of empire cries out for demystification, he writes, because although we are no longer in it, we don't know how much of it is still in us.

So it is with the miners' strike. Unreliable though our memories may be, it still remains very much a part of who we are. And so it should be, for all of us.

Many people have helped me in various ways to produce this volume and I thank them all. I am going to list as many of them as I can possibly remember, though if anyone finds they have been omitted it is more a measure of my stupidity than lack of gratitude.

First of all the interviewees. Each of them gave up their time to speak to a stranger asking them questions about a vital part of their lives. Without exception they did so with generosity and openness and without them there would be no book. As with all the others mentioned here, they have no responsibility for any views expressed in the introduction. For better or worse, they are solely mine. To Professor John Foster, Richard Leonard, Carolyn Mack, Dave

Greaves, Ron McKay, Ronnie Stevenson, Dennis O'Donnell, Jim Murray, Marion Sinclair, Jackie Gulstad, Alex Murphy, the staff at Glasgow's Mitchell Library, Fife and Lothian Regional Council staff and those of West Lothian, Midlothian, and Cumnock and Doon Valley District Councils, and the Coalfield Communities Campaign – many thanks.

Above all, I owe to my wife, Liz Catterson, and son, Patrick, an immeasurable debt and it is to them both that I dedicate this book.

Joe Owens

AYRSHIRE

HELEN GRAY

Cumnock

At the moment I'm working full time as a bar steward. Usually I just do part-time. When the strike started I was actually working in a hotel in Cumnock, part-time, dayshift, seven to eleven in the morning. It was awkward to start with; my man was going out on the picket line. It was a bit awkward because I was up early, he was up early and the kids were quite young at the time. Anyway we got roon aboot that problem.

The women mair or less started going up tae the strike centre to help wi' the meals, make sandwiches up and make the dinners. As the strike progressed, women being women, they started to make decisions and it wasnae accepted too well tae start wi'. We were putting our noses in saying they should have been daein this and they should have been daein that.

But we organised a women's picket, maybe a month tae six weeks intae the strike. Just women. An' we went oot wi' oor banners an' oor placards tae the Killoch and actually turned every fireman, oversman, a' the officials that day and we got a guid reception when we came back fae the men. So I think they appreciated then we had a place.

I don't know whether it was psychological that the men wouldnae walk by women or whether they thought we were making a better point than the men were daein. We won a victory that day and fae then on it was really hell for leather.

I was getting up and going out on the picket before I went tae my work at seven, gaun straight tae my work fae the picket line. As it progressed we just got intae a routine. We got organised intae a women's committee, got rotas made up for the meals, crèches for watching the weans. Then the invitations were coming in, there was a bus going to Yorkshire or a bus going to London so we just drew the names out. Me, I had never been to London, some o' the lassies had never been oot o' Scotland and that aspect of it was good, it broadened their horizons, it broadened our horizons. Meeting different people, seeing different places, getting involved.

It made you politically aware, really. In a wee sleepy place like this you just went tae the supermarket and did your shopping. If anybody was working she had a wee part-time job and that was really your world. You read the papers and watched the news but we felt didnae really affect us. But that a' changed and we reopened the local Labour Party in the area wi' the members oot the strike centre. It had been closed for a few years.

Eventually they sent for delegates from all areas for a national women's committee and that's really when the big move went on as far as the women were concerned. I mean, they got cash in and started going to big conferences – Sheffield, London and getting really, really involved at top level. We were always asked for a women's speaker at every rally or meeting and we had local women on the same platform as Arthur Scargill and Neil Kinnock and the big names.

It was frightening for housewives that had never been used tae public speaking tae get up there and dae their bit but they did it. We even had lassies gettin' sent tae Belfast, Queen's College, tae address a rally. I was at Belfast masel, but it was an open air rally. It was on the back o' a trailer and ma knees were shaking. A' they things were the good points, broadening the lassies' horizons and making us mair politically aware. That was great.

The bad points. Well, it broke up a lot o' families. There were rifts in ma ain family because ma brother was a fireman*. He felt he was just daein his job, because he wasnae on strike, they had to keep the pit open. He wouldnae walk by me. If I was on the picket line he wouldnae walk by me. But as I say, it caused a lot o' rifts.

The financial side o' it was just a nightmare, an absolute nightmare. The debt we got intae wasnae real. But everybody was in the same boat though and it didnae really matter. I don't know how to explain it. You knew everybody was the same so we didnae girn and greet aboot it. We just got on wi' it an' we shared what we had. We had a lot o' good nights, the women. The cheapest bottle o' wine you could afford, or even a bottle o' cider an' it a' went intae a big tub wi' fruit, wi' oranges and apples. We scoffed that and had a sing-song and a greet many a night, but that was maybe once a month we did that wi' the women fae the strike centre.

One o' the other things that came oot o' that was that in oor local club up there, where I'm working the noo, there's a games room, there's a lounge and there's a dance hall. The games room was always predominantly men. I had never been in the games room, I couldnae tell you what it looked like. And of course it was a summer like this,

* A pit deputy

a really hot summer. About four or five o' us came oot o' the kitchen when we finished washing up an' that, after the meal was by and said – we'll go for a shandy, we'll go through tae the games room and see what the men are cooking up for the night; is there anything happening the night or whatever. And that was the first for a long, long time they had seen women in the games room. And we were welcomed wi' open arms. And noo it's no' a man's games room. Some nights it's predominantly women that's in it. There's naebody turns their head noo when a woman walks intae the games room.

Towards the end o' it everybody was getting really, really fed up. We thought we were never going to see the end o' this. They knew they werenae gaun tae win anything, they knew by then but we had some stubborn ones here that wouldnae go back and we had some sacked boys tae. When it did finally happen everybody was glad in a way, kenning you were getting back tae your work but it was sad, it was really sad because I think everybody knew you would never have that again, that closeness, camaraderie and everybody sticking thegether. You knew that was coming tae an end.

It was really sad to lose the company and for a few weeks if there was a mothers' and toddlers' meeting the same lassies would be there or if there was a guild meeting the aulder women would be there and they were still talking aboot it and we'll need to organise something else tae keep a' the women thegether that had been there. But it never ever materialised because, of course, when everybody went back tae their work this materialistic thing came back intae it – oh, they're working noo, we have had a year without a wage and I need a new suite, I need a new carpet. And the brilliant ideas that they sat and spoke aboot when they had nae money just went oot the windae. Cannae blame them in a way, but it was sad tae see that breaking doon because they had a really strong committee up there at one time.

But noo I wouldnae hesitate, in fact we were talking aboot it last week, if it hadnae been for the way he works we were gaun tae go tae Dundee tae support the Timex workers. I wouldnae hesitate to go and support anybody in struggle for a just cause. No' just in the trade union movement, anything. That's what's been instilled in me. I think – we've been there, we've been at the other end o' the stick so you just want tae show a wee bit o' appreciation tae other folk because there were a lot o' people good tae us. The strike's changed my feelings that way.

Another thing, I wouldnae walk by anybody wi' a can in their hand noo that's collecting for anything, because I was there tae. We had it a'. I think there were a lot o' valuable lessons learned. It would've been better if everybody had stuck thegether after the strike but the momentum wasnae there, there was nothing tae fight for, so we just drifted away.

To be quite honest I wouldnae have said boo tae a mouse before the strike. Noo I'll stand my ground wi' anybody, management, anybody, I don't care who they are. If I know I'm right and I've got rights, whether it be in a workplace, in a shop or wherever, before I would have walked away and accepted a no or a sorry, noo I'll no'. It's made me stronger that way.

During the strike we were a' scared for oor television licences, there was no way we could pay it. And one o' the women that supported us, her husband worked for BT, he went oot on one of the detector vans. And a' she said was – open your door and tell him – you're no' getting in. I says – you cannae dae that, she says – aye you can, you don't need tae let them in your house. Now, we didnae know these things. I mean we picked up a lot o' tips like that.

But if you sit doon and think about it, we're getting trod on a' the time. It's what we don't know that's making us walk away fae things. If we knew the rights and the wrongs and the ins and the outs we would fight back and say we're no' daein this and we're no' daein that.

My eldest boy, he was the first YTS employee o' the National Coal Board in Scotland, when they started employing YTS after the strike.

When they were shutting Killoch, they offered him a transfer tae Wales. He was only seventeen, so there was no way he was going to Wales, so he packed it in. But he loved it, that boy loved his job. He's noo at Glasgow University doing a business studies course. But he's had that world o' experience working in a pit.

I would say that nae more than twenty or thirty miners that were on strike have noo got a job in Netherthird, and there are about 111 families. There's nae light industry here at a', nothing, and that makes them apathetic tae. I mean, if they had a job the fight would probably come back but the majority's no' working and it knocks the stuffing out o' them.

In the social club where I'm working we have boys coming in there, and I'm talking about boys aged twenty-four and twenty-five and they have never worked fae they left the school. And that's them intae a routine. They come up to the club every morning, have a can o' juice and play cards fae twelve o'clock tae three in the afternoon and that is their daily routine. Never worked. And I don't think they ever will work. It's the long term unemployed. Whereas if these two pits had still a been gaun, Killoch and the Barony, those boys would all have jobs, no' just in the pits but in other related industries.

We had Fenners doon here that made the belts for the pits, that's closed as well. The place has been decimated, totally. You'd find that in Auchinleck, I'll bet, because there were a lot mair miners there than here.

I think if the women's meetings had carried on and got a wee bit o' encouragement I think I would've went into local politics. I was on the register; I was vetted for going on the register for a councillor but, as I say, it's hard to go to these meeting yourself. If there were two or three o' you, fine, somebody to gie you a wee bit o' a push, but that fell through.

I regret it because we got quite a few things done. OK, it was maybe for the benefit o' women. We got toilets put in the local shopping precinct. It's quite a big precinct and the only toilets were away doon at the other end o' the town, and we kept bringing this up and bringing this up. If you're daein the shopping and you've got two weans wi' you, you've to trek shopping a' the way down to the other end o' the town for a wean to go to the toilet. We finally got toilets put into the precinct, that was one good thing. We got two or three local things done wi' the council and it's a shame that that's no' there now to get especially women's issues over.

I can remember one day the Provost of Paisley had made a donation, a cheque. Three o' us went to a big supermarket in Paisley. It was wrong at the time because we should have gone to a warehouse, we were shopping for twelve strike centres. It was a publicity stunt, STV were there following us round about filling the trolleys.

We were just going forward to the checkout and this wee old pensioner came up to me wi' half a dozen eggs and she was greetin. She says – it's no' much, it's a' I can afford but take that for your strike centre. And see when the film came out, it was on the six o'clock news that night, I was emptying the trolley and the big guy fae STV was asking me what it was like tae beg for donations, but they never showed the clip o' that auld women, greetin, giving me the half a dozen eggs – that was too sympathetic, that was going tae get the public on the side o' the miners through television and they couldnae dae that because the media was a' against us.

Before, we believed everything we read in the papers, believed everything we saw on the television but after that strike we knew what was what.

RAB GRAY

Cumnock

In this area there is nothing. Miners grew up, followed their father, they didnae ken nothing else so they cannae go and get a job. Good workers, but naebody's going to employ them whereas I was in and out the pit and I've turned my hand tae certain things. I'm one o' the fortunate ones but most o' them didnae have a chance, never had a chance because there's nothing there to teach them anything.

It's alright tae say there's courses and that but there's still no' a job at the end o' the line. It's the government keeping the figures doon. As I say, I'm one o' the lucky yins, lucky in a way and unlucky because what's happened is the employers are keeping you tae the minimum. You cannae fight them, they just show you the gate.

You either take what they give you or forget it. My employer, and I don't care if he ever reads the book, says he's a Labour man. He's no' tae me. He's a Tory through and through as far as I'm concerned.

In this area I cannae say the men are much different fae before, men who stuck the strike like me. We still help yin another.

Say if you wanted something done, you couldnae afford it but you needed it done, the boys that were involved in the strike a' get thegether. But the men that went back are entirely different. They must find it different, they must feel they are still locked up because it was bitter here. They never show face in that club. They drop their heads when they walk by you. We're talking about ten years noo. But so far as this community's concerned everybody still helps one another. They wouldnae see you stuck. I dare say it's the same in every other area.

I would be getting two and a half times the wages I'm getting noo if I was still in the pit. Guaranteed. I had a good wage in the pit. I did mine driving, I worked the face line. I'd have a lot mair money than what I have at the present moment.

The place has deteriorated. It was a' one big area, the villages an' that. There was plenty tae dae, there was wee works like Fenners. Folk had still tae travel tae Kilmarnock but it was a' tae dae wi' railways, it was a' tae dae wi' the pits. They're no' there noo so it shut the factories as well forby shutting the pit. At that time when the pits were gaun this was a great area all over here. Noo it has deteriorated. Folk don't want tae move, they've been here a' their life. My middle boy cannae get a job, I wouldnae move fae here just tae get him a job.

When the pits were gaun we used tae run buses tae Wembley and things like that but you cannae dae that any more because the boys arenae working, they've no money. We used tae have Gomber here, who make the trucks. A year they were here. A lot o' boys learned skills for that but where can they take them noo? There's nothing for them. There's nae long-term prospects.

It's a' opencast that's round about here noo and it's machines that dae the work. Say the council makes an agreement wi' them that they'll employ x amount of labour fae this area, there might be only thirty folk working at an opencast so they might only have tae employ ten. That's it.

Noo I'm no' afraid tae ask for my rights instead o' just taking what they say. No' that it gets you anywhere, mind you. Regarding the state that the country's in, the big boys have got the ba' at their foot and they're going tae kick it. You can't win, but you can say a lot mair than you could then because you've learned a lot mair.

I'm still bitter tae this day. There are folk I'll never speak tae, never. In fact they stay two doors along fae me. Never. The boy next door was NACODS and I had it oot wi' him.

The way they went about it they were actually laughing at you. They were going hame wi' a wage every week, you werenae. If they were gaun oot at the weekend, where were you? You were maybe picketing a power station like Hunterston. I mean we were there a' weekend.

There's people I'll never speak tae. Two or three maybe, but the biggest majority of them, no. They don't exist. They didn't help me, not one little bit.

I don't see a future as far as work's concerned, no' the same as when the pits were gaun. Pits were the backbone in every area and they brought industry tae areas. As long as there were pits, other bits moved in. Nae pits, they move out.

I would go through it again. It just showed how strong a bond there was among folk, how it brought folk thegether. I've seen us sitting up in the club having a good blether about it, things that were funny, things that werenae funny, but just talking about it. I would go back tae the pit in a minute. A different class o' people tae work wi'. You look after one another. Out in this world it's man mind thyself, doon the pit you looked after yin another.

BILLY HODGE

Cumnock

I live in Cumnock. I have done for the past twelve years. I'm now in my second marriage. I've got two older kids fae my first marriage and two wee ones fae my second marriage.

Basically speaking, going to the pits was the easy road out. A' ma folks were in the pits, a' I'd ever heard o' was pits and there was loads of them round about here, it was just the in thing. That was where you went if you were aff a mining family. My family, my brothers, my full family was in the pits so that's where I went. I started an engineering apprenticeship in August 1968 an' I finished up on December 28, '85.

I was really, really involved in the strike. I wasnae sort o' involved in the union as such at the pit. This area's always been big on strike centres, like '72 and '74 there was always a big strike centre here. I got involved early on an' I was secretary o' the strike centre.

I saw it as the be all and end all because although I wasnae involved in the union as such, I was quite political an' I took a lot o' interest in what people said an' I thought Scargill actually came ten years too late. That was a personal view.

I didnae think a great deal o' the hierarchy o' the NUM in this area or my particular union SCEBTA. I thought they let people get on wi' things rather than gie them a bit o' direction and actually, rightly or wrongly, I thought we put a lot more into the strike than they actually did at Netherthird strike centre, which was the main one outside the NUM office in Ayr.

We did a lot more organising during the strike an' it became a sort o' power struggle, a mini power struggle. They didnae like what we told them. As far as we were led to believe doon here, throughout Scotland there were six main areas, six main strike centres. There was Ayr, Fallin an' I don't just remember the others, an' that all the funds that came into Scotland were split up six ways. We felt that was really unjust because, in the Fallin area, we didnae know how many men were involved up there, but we knew it was much less. We had about four and a half thousand men doon here and they had nothing like that and we fought that.

About a week into the strike we got visitors, like Militant and the Socialist Workers Party and we were clearly told you do not get involved wi' the 'banana bunch', that sort o' thing, to which we told them [the hierarchy] 'piss off'. If this was the way the strike was going to be run then we'll run it as we see fit an' we'll finance our ain efforts personally.

The organisation was really, really good. We had, in Netherthird and Craigens, just two wee housing schemes, 134 striking miners who had to be catered for in one way or another. We thought that the NUM in Ayr, who sat in their chairs and signed this bit o' paper and that bit o' paper, couldnae compute that we had to deal wi' this and so a power struggle evolved. They didnae like how we were. We said – it's our bodies that're on the line, our conscience that's on the line and you can basically, go away, or words to that effect.

It came to be that they came a lot tae us up here an' asked how do you feel about this, should this be OK. It came that we became the power then. They seemed to be comfortable sitting in their office an' as far as I'm led to believe they were picking up their wages every week as full-time NUM members, which didnae go down a bomb I can assure you. We were being assured that anything over and above the basic living standard was being put into the funds but personally speaking I just don't believe it.

I appreciated the help that we got fae people, there's a couple sticks in my mind. There's a Chivas Regal place, I think it's in Paisley Road an' it was a John McGee. I went an' spoke to him a couple o' times an' the guy looked as if he didnae care, as if he didnae hae a care in the world.

But the things that guy did for us were unreal. Just up to a couple o' years ago I got Christmas cards from him. Super guy. The Militant, their organisation and the back up we got from them was tremendous. Obviously they know how tae go about things. It was mainly younger folk who were involved on the strike committee an' we hadnae the wherewithal because we hadnae been involved in previous strikes which were shorter affairs anyway. The contacts they had were brilliant an' we financed our strike through them.

Initially we hadnae nobody working an' it was absolutely brilliant. Out o' the 130 men who were on strike fae the two wee housing schemes here there were 97 active in the strike. There was others who didnae want to go picketing an' we said that was fine but the pulling together o' the whole community was brilliant. We had pensioners, the minister, everybody coming in an' wishing us well. The strike centre was open twenty-four hours a day an' if anybody had any particular problems there was always usually somebody there to advise them or at least listen. At the finish-up about seven men went back to work out o' these two housing schemes about nine months into the strike. We had later ones, like a week before the end o' the strike, which I'll never understand, but it was apparent we were all pulling together.

I feel it pretty bad now that the strike's over I can walk into the club and people you had been like brothers wi' for a year gie a nod on the way by. It's just fell to bits, it really has. The camaraderie's gone, it's just non-existent now. There's nae focal point tae anything now. The guys I was on strike wi' that, as I said, appeared like my brothers, we were so close. But even when we werenae on strike I was still working wi these guys and had mair contact. Now the only time you see them is if you pass them in the street or go for a pint. The contact's no' there. The place is dead, basically speaking.

I'm very, very cynical. Bitter. Really, really bitter. That's about the political scene as a whole an' the political scene locally an' the people I was involved wi'. I feel really, really bitter about it. The guys that went back to work, I don't understand how they could. After being on strike for nine months just gi'ing up like that. I ken everybody's no' built the same way and don't have the same beliefs. Mind you, I didnae think I had the belief to begin wi', that I would've been on strike that length o' time. But I've become so much more politically aware, very watchful of whom I associate with. I don't trust anybody anymore. It'd take a long, long time before I'd trust anybody.

When I went back in March, I had been constant dayshift, they told me you're nightshift this week, backshift next week. I said fine, they're getting back at us for the strike. So I just accepted that. Our gaffer was actually a very good guy. He actually put his son out the house because he was the second guy back at Killoch pit. He pulled me into the office and told me to get the hell's fire out of the pit as soon as I could, 'cause there wasnae any way I would last a year. He said there was one guy in particular, a deputy chief engineer, he says he's made it quite clear that he's gonnae follow you, he's gonnae check a' your work, he's just gunnin' for you.

Various things happened. They were really forcing you into situations. There were certain sections that they didnae send scab workers intae, it was just 'Tuesday Boys' an' I was never sent into one o' them. I was always pushed in among the scabs. For about three months I never held a conversation doon the pit at all, never spoke to a single soul. I always remember I got wet one day an' I got an early lousing line for being wet an' that deputy chief engineer followed me right out an' checked my line five times between leaving work and getting to the surface. I just thought to myself – get out quick wi' something rather than wi' nothing. The opportunity arose an' I took it. I don't feel any regret at all about doing it.

I was unemployed for three months then I applied for a job as a swimming pool supervisor at the local swimming pool, it's open air an' it's only open during the summer. I did that for that summer season then I worked wi' a wee engineering company. Then I was back in in the summer season o' '87 at the swimming pool and the people that I'm working wi' now came in and I got involved wi' them, it was the mentally handicapped fae Auchinleck Adult Training Centre. When the summer season at the swimming pool finished I was at a loose end an' they asked me if I would be interested in doing voluntary work an' I said aye. I was doing voluntary work two or three days a week.

I was sitting in the house one Friday an' one o' the guys arrived at the house and says – you've to come out to Auchinleck. So I went out an' it was the manager who said – just fill this form in – it was an application for a temporary contract. So I got a temporary contract there then we moved into a purpose-built place in Cumnock. I got two temporary contracts there an' then I got started as a full-time instructor. Shortly after that Jane started an' that's been us since.

There's quite a bit o' industry in the area gone, everything.

They're bringing in small factory units. There's no employment. Nothing. Absolutely nothing. There's nothing to make it a community again. I doubt very much if there can be anything made o' it again.

My principles don't change. There've been strikes where I work, where it's been a national day of action thing, and I've totally disagreed wi' them an' I didn't go on strike. But if exactly the same set o' circumstances arose again (1984/85) then I would. I would definitely go through it again. I would have more consideration for my family, though, because they were totally deserted during the strike. I don't think I would be that heavily involved now that I gave up that amount of time. I don't think I would take the risks I took during that strike. I'm a wee bit older and a wee bit wiser.

I'm a proud man, I think. I don't think I've anything to be proud o' lasting out a year on strike, I think that was necessary for what I believed in. But I feel proud that I did my best. It maybe wasnae guid enough, but I did my best. For everybody. I don't think it was appreciated as much as it should've been, I don't know.

Pits has been the way o' life here for everybody, even people who werenae in the pits. People that owned the pubs made money fae the miners. The people who owned shops earned money fae the miners. It's all gone. The wee corner shop doon there at the weekend is open two hours. God almighty, corner shops everywhere are opened tae ten o'clock at night. It's just naebody's got any money.

I count myself as a very fortunate man in what I've got now. But there's nothing in the future, not that I can foresee anyhow. If you're looking for a future, this is no' the place to look.

YVONNE HODGE

Cumnock

I'm nineteen an' I've got a wee boy named Rees and my boyfriend Rab.

Being nine I didnae ken that much about it [the strike] but I thought it was brilliant because we got holidays and we got our free dinners at the community centre and things like that. I didnae realise the effects it would have on families and things like that because I was only nine. It must have been a year of hell for families because they had no money.

During the strike folk whose dads werenae working in the pit were getting new trainers and clothes and everything like that – that we couldnae get – and I just couldnae understand why we couldnae get them.

My pal's dad went back to his work and I thought we would get stopped seeing each other but the man came and said to my father about me and Claire, about it no' affecting our friendship because we were the best o' pals. It didnae. Just because my father and him werenae talking didnae mean me and Claire couldnae talk.

It rubbed off on the weans, like me calling folk scabs and things like that. I just kent that a scab was somebody that went back to work when they shouldnae because it was a strike and probably if the scabs hadnae went back to work the miners would have won. You got the weans' fathers that were on strike and the weans' fathers that went back and there was a lot o' hassle for the weans' fathers that went back, 'cause they were getting cried scabs as well.

I mind my father sitting in the kitchen greetin' and I didnae really understand what he was greetin' for but he said that that was them beat. No' long after that he got made redundant.

I still see folk on the street and say he was a scab and he wasnae. The folk that I run about wi' during the strike, like, we were all the best o' pals, I hardly see any o' them now. I really don't now that they've got their different lives and all that. I actually see very little o' them.

There's a lot o' folk I ken on the broo who just cannae get work. I suppose if the pits had still been open there would have been a lot more jobs. It's terrible, there's absolutely nothing. You've got tae go tae Ayr or Kilmarnock for work and most times there's nae work there either so you get a load o' folk moving away to England and abroad to try and get work.

Young people have nothing to dae but hang about the streets, that's basically it. If you go tae the nearest sports centre you've got to pay to get in but folk have nae money an' cannae pay to get into it.

I was working until I left to have the wean. I was working in a private nursing home in Kilmarnock, but it was only part-time. It doesnae pay me to go back because it's only part-time and really terrible wages. I would be worse off than I am the now. I had £16 bus fares to pay and I only earned £45 to £50 a week. It pays me no' to work.

At the moment I'm waiting for a house which is taking forever because they just don't care. It's those you know. But once we get a house I'm hoping things'll pick up. I'm hoping to go back to work but me and Rab would have to have good paying jobs for it to benefit us.

Some of my pals have been lucky, like, have done YT Schemes and have been kept on but there's a lot o' them on the broo because they cannae get work.

Off my wages and Rab's broo money we had to try an' put away what we could to try and save up for a house but it's basically impossible on what we earn, what we get the now. So we've got practically nothing tae move in wi'. I stay wi' my dad. We were staying wi' Rab's mum but there's absolutely nae room there; but it's overcrowded here as well. We really, really need to get out and get our own place.

There's nothing here. You've got to have good experience and Highers and 'O' Levels but even if you dae stay on at school you're still no' guaranteed a job. Most o' my pals have got families or are on the broo. Basically some o' them had families so they can get money, a house and things like that. I don't see things getting better; I just see things getting worse.

DANNY GEMMEL

Auchinleck

I was a miner for twelve years. I started the pit on my seventeenth birthday and I went through the strike in '84 and I finished in the colliery in 1988.

My first experience o' strikes was just one-day affairs and then came '84. It went half-cocked because we never got the actual support o' a' our union as it stood at the time. I thought it was run the wrong way from the top but at that time we thought strike was a feasible way to fight for better rights, better pay, better working conditions.

It was good during the strike because there was plenty unity, every other union supported us but tae me it was a futile exercise once the year was up because everybody was gaun back tae their work because they started tae see through it; that it was just a waste o' time and a waste o' money.

I went back in February, about three weeks before it finished, but it was by wi' then. I was sitting here in the strike centre and the television was on and Arthur Scargill came on and he says we'll be out another year so that just finished most o' the boys in here.

We were rock bottom at that time anyway, morale was low. Most o' the boys had gone back in dribs and drabs through the days and we were a' like brothers in here and tae see your pals gaun back, something just wasnae there for the fight anymore.

A' the boys really that were left were the boys who had been sacked through picketing and that was it. Looking back now I would say it was a year's wages lost. Men never, ever recouped they wages and never, ever will. We fought for jobs and tae me the local communities and collieries and that were shut politically because we were hard militant at the time, everybody was militant and it was a hard nut to crack but they cracked it here in Ayrshire.

Do I regret the strike? Morally no, financially yes. I had a bad year that year. I lost a child tae. Falling out between families which was nae guid, bad blood between a lot o' the families. It was a learning process for me. As I say I had never been òn strike before but you know who your friends and who your brothers are and to me, miners, we're a different breed o' people because we a' stick thegether through thick and thin.

I never, ever regretted gaun back tae my work. As I say, most o' the boys were gaun back at the time anyway, but there was never any bad feeling about it in this area. Looking back, the full community's decimated now, it's a ghost town. There's nae future for any o' the young yins, nae jobs, just a wasteland. But I blame the government.

It's a' politics, that's a' it boils doon tae at the finish-up and we're only the pawns on the chessboard. That's how I look at it myself.

When the pits were open in this area there were jobs, there was money, the economy was guid, everybody was prospering. Young yins that were coming up that were leaving the school, they were getting jobs. Noo, I deal wi' young yins round about the village when I work in the community centre and a' they live for now is drugs and alcohol, no' jobs. It's a waste. They're a wasted generation, this generation anyway, the teenagers. They've nae prospects for anything, nothing tae look forward tae so they go about vandalising, ken.

It's actually sad in a way tae see the village gaun like that inside maybe six years. I remember what it used tae be like. Pubs, clubs, a' them tae, they're no' the same either. You used tae have tae queue up at the workmen's club tae get in at five o'clock some nights. See noo, you can get in anytime.

Everybody suffered through the strike, richt doon through the chain. Shops have shut, a lot o' bits boarded up in Auchinleck. It used to be a thriving community but you cannae turn the clock back noo.

I'm very bitter towards the Tory Government. When I see what's being imported noo in coal, putting their ain people oot o' jobs, that's the galling bit about it. I cannae fathom politics oot for that. An it's a' yin how much we rant and rave, we cannae dae nothing about it. We tried our best in '84 and that was it.

After the pit shut in '88 I was a year unemployed. I got a job in a factory doon in Irvine for a year. I had a young family tae support, everything was going ok. I had already spent my redundancy money in the year prior tae that, that was away so I was glad tae get a job. Then, two days after Christmas in '91, I was paid off. That was me another year on the broo and then, finally I did a course in youth education looking after young yins and I finally ended up in the community centre in Auchinleck and I'm hoping to be here for a while.

So I was yin o' the lucky yins in Auchinleck but a lot o' boys I worked wi' have never, ever worked fae the pit shut and are never, ever likely tae work for there's nae need for miners noo. See, that was a skill.

I've worked in factories and different environments and it's no' the same camaraderie or anything, ken – I'll watch your back and you watch mine. It's a' backstabbing noo. They're a different breed o' people as far as I'm concerned. They're maybe Scottish but they're no' the same. No' the same unions. If you show you're militant o' any kind noo in any factory, you're straight out the door. If you voice your opinion that's you. You've got tae be a yes man, three bags full man and that's it.

I found that through experience. I think that's how I lost my job up there. In fact there were six miners a' got paid off thegether so that tells you a thing or two.

A lot o' boys went doon tae England, I've two brothers that went tae work in the pits doon there. My other brother's a surveyor at the opencast but he worked in Killoch since he was a boy. He went tae university and got his surveying papers. It was a' miners in the house. My dad was a miner, my grandpas. It was a' mining stock. It was the only thing that was for us and that was it. It was just a way o' life for us. It was a Monday tae Friday job and we were happy.

But I'd go back tomorrow. I'd pack this in and go back tomorrow. You ken the people you're working wi'. I miss it, everybody, a' the miners dae. It's the first thing you dae, if you're gaun oot for a night, you're sitting talking away, it's the first thing – by Christ I miss the pit, miss the patter and the banter. Everybody worked thegether, everybody worked in a unit. It's no' the same up and elsewhere. They've killed that noo, it'll never be the same noo. But life goes on and you've just tae struggle on.

I suppose it's just a part o' life, innit.. You've got tae hae your ups and doons and I would say mair doons than ups. If you're trying tae bring up a young family and you think your job's safe for life when you go in the pit, it's a gut wrench.

You can see the waste. There's millions and millions o' tons o' coal in this area alone. Different countries would be exploiting that. When you see the waste and money that's been left doon a pit, for instance. I worked in two pits in this area, Highhouse and Barony, and the stuff that's been left doon's criminal. As far as I'm concerned it's criminal. Million and millions o' pounds o' stuff just buried and left.

Then the government talks about wastage. They're actually spending mair money keeping miners on the dole instead o' producing coal at a profitable price. It'll come in twenty or thirty years they'll need to open them back up but where will they get the miners fae in Scotland then? The skills will have gone. I could go back tae the face tomorrow and be fine, but in twenty years I cannae.

This area's been decimated. I'll be quite honest with you, if it wasnae for Auchinleck Talbot this would be a ghosttown. The football team gies the folk in Auchinleck a lift every year and that's no' kidding. And that's it, nothing else.

DAVE MAGUIRE

Auchinleck

I first started work as a coachbuilder and I lasted a fortnight. It was the summer an' you werenae getting home tae six o'clock so I says that'll dae me so I just packed it in and finished up in the pit. I went for an interview on the Friday and they told me to start on the Monday. I worked in the pits for thirty-four year. I quite liked it at times, ken. It was a guid job, I quite enjoyed it.

The strike was a hard, dour struggle I can tell you. It was hard on the wife but I had a boy who was working which helped a lot, gave us a good hand. It was a hard, dour struggle but you got good times tae, many a laugh and it was the best summer ever we had. I stayed out the full year. They started back on the Tuesday morning and I didnae start tae the following Tuesday.

I see now that the coal board were wanting a fight. They were wanting a battle. They didnae care about pits, they were after unions, they were after the strongest union tae. It was a war for unions that's what they were after.

The pit could have went on wi' two hundred men, young men. It would have done this village, there's nothing here noo. Scargill told us in ten year we would hardly have a village; it's about five I've been off noo and there's nothing below the brig, there's no' even a shop and if there's anything opening it's a Chinky restaurant or a vindaloo or something.

O'er at Highhouse they say it's an industrial estate there, there's no' a hundred workers. There's nae future in the village; I mean there's nothing here and there's nae use saying there is because there's nothing, definitely nae future for young men about here.

There is a change. If we hadnae the fitba' team we would have nothing. It's only Talbot that's keeping this place and if they go down they'll go quick because the money's no there, the money's no there tae keep them gaun. You've hardly enough tae keep yourself gaun wi' what you've got.

Before, you had a tear, you had two or three bob and you had people going holidays here and there but everybody's o' the same opinion noo that we're finished, ken. When the pit shut in '62 we thought it was finished but we kent there was maybe jobs. Where dae you move tae noo? You cannae even move for jobs, there's nae jobs for you.

When the strike finished I was on the broo for a year. I applied for a hundred jobs, in fact I didnae bother applying any more. I went for a course at bricking and here when I got there it was a' miners that were there and it was really brilliant. I thoroughly enjoyed it. So I left the bricking course and got a job as a labourer and I was labouring for six months and I thoroughly enjoyed it then I got paid off and I've no' had a job since then. That was 1990.

I miss the pit, definitely. I miss the company. Bit o' tear, bit o' patter. The folk I felt sorry for during the strike was the boys that got sacked. There's a boy here in Auchinleck got fined £30,000 for daein nothing and there's folk running about breaking into houses get two years community service. That boy won his case. He got about £9,000 and the Assistance took £5,000 back aff him because he was a year on the assistance. Instead o' £34,000 he got £4,000. He was a head yin during the strike, that's what it was, they were just after him and they got him.

I'm more restless, depression, what dae you dae? You get up in the morning, where are you gaun? Gaun for a walk? Where are you gaunny go in the afternoon if it's raining? You just lie in the house, go tae your bed. It changes your life. You get, och, you just don't bother. Life's no' the same actually, it's no' really, ken.

I'd like a job but I'm no' saying pits noo because I'm too old for them. I'd like a job at the labouring again. But, och, it's definitely no' the same, no' the same atmosphere, the village is no' the same. Everybody's a' for theresel noo, everybody fends for number one before they do anything noo.

I don't like it mind you but I've just got into the rut and that's it. I started gardening when I left the pit but I'm even saying I'll get that the morn tae. The first two year you want tae dae everything and now you cannae be bothered.

If I was a young man I would move away, but where would you go? I cannae see any future in Auchinleck at a' nor nae mining village. They'll never find jobs for 4000 in this locality, no way. So I'm finished for life, I'm by working for life. I've just gave up the fight at a', I'm just going along, son, just tae get the time in.

And our MP, I don't know what he does at a'. Stays doon there in a £100,000 house, doesnae ken what's gaun on. He's no' a bad fellow but you have to be among your ain tae see what's gaun on, tae see what the position is. There's mair crime noo in this village than ever there was and there's nae police. Plenty o' them during the strike right enough.

I'm bitter against the boys that started back early but them that started back late, no, because the game was by anyway. In fact I thought Scargill should have blew the whistle before he did and maybe we could have had another go.

You used tae get ten redundant men doon at the corner waiting tae go for a walk. I walk two dogs and noo you never see a soul. I don't know what they dae, they must lie about. They're no' the same. They're no' walking the same or nothing like that. Our village is away, Scargill said ten years, and that's only five and that's it.

I was quite active before. I was always on the union, I was always doon at the bowling, the fitba' committee and things like that, I don't even bother noo. I just let it be noo.

FIFE

PAT RATTRAY

Kelty

I live in a village in Fife called Kelty. It's a village that's been built up on mining; there were a lot o' pits around here. Unfortunately, there's nae pits in Kelty now. The men that work in Kelty, bar a few, have tae travel out for work.

I'm still working in the pits. I'm a mechanical engineer tae trade and I'm a union official at Castlebridge Colliery which is in the Longannet Complex. It was a pit that was opened after the strike, in September '86 and it's still going well. Hopefully it'll go well intae the next century.

I started in the pits in October 1977. I wasnae like a lot o' the lads who have been in the pit since they left the school, I was what you could call a late starter in the pit, I started when I was thirty years old. I started at Castlehill mine which you could say was part o' the Longannet Complex because a' the coal fae Castlehill went on the common belt tae Longannet. At that time, Castlehill, Bogside and Solsgirth a' fed on tae the one belt and a' that coal went tae Longannet Power Station.

Coming up tae the strike we had a couple o' token overtime bans and you could see something was coming. In '84 there was the call for a strike and I think there was a couple o' pits oot before us. Seafield was out maybe a week before us. But before that you could see it was a' boiling underneath and I didnae think we were going tae get any settlement wi' British Coal, I couldnae see that.

When the strike started we seemed tae be lost; we seemed tae be in limbo for a while and then we started tae get organised and got a strike centre in Kelty. We came under the area strike centre at Fishcross. A man who lives in the village, a bit o' a character, Archie Campbell, he helped us set the strike centre up and we set it up in the club.

We used tae have our meetings in Kelty Ex-Servicemen's Club and then later on we had them in a pub doon the road. It was called Number One and that was where we used tae have a' our meals and everything. That was when we got organised.

When the strike started tae go on and on and on we were called tae go picketing. The first picket was just outside Dunfermline. There was a wee coal plant there. It was only a token picket. And then, at some time every week we had tae provide pickets for Longannet Power Station and Kincardine Power Station tae the extent that they pickets were there twenty-four hours and they put a caravan at each one.

Odd days, maybe two or three days a week, we would go away picketing tae different places. We were at Dundee, we were at Hunterston and we were just at oor ain pits, Solsgirth, Castlehill, these sort o' things. And then we were at the big pickets as the year went on. I was at the big picket at Orgreave and everything like that.

I think our main goal throughout the strike was tae try and keep ourselves as a group. At that time in Kelty I would say we had well over a hundred miners, but in saying that we could only maintain a hard core o' about forty, maybe fifty that would come for meals, go picketing and things like that.

When we decided tae get ourselves really set up we had a chairman and a secretary, I was the treasurer and my wife was the treasurer o' the ladies group.

It was a hard year but I was fortunate in the fact that my wife backed me up. I know a lot o' boys who didnae get that support fae their wives. I mean during the strike, fae the Social, I got eleven pounds a week and that was for the four of us. That kept four o' us and that was it, that was a' we got. My mother and my old aunt used tae gie us a bit pound a week, because my brother was on strike as well.

It was hard, but looking back on it I dinnae regret one bit of it, like. We got told that a' the money we got fae the Social we wouldnae have tae pay it back, but we did have tae pay it back. I paid a' mine back. I just took a conscious decision that I would take it on and pay it a' back.

I enjoyed it. It's like everything else, after it's finished you miss it. I was in the jail twice and I was warned no' tae go back on the picket line. And I can remember one day, the second time I got lifted, I actually was charged. I came home and I said tae her that I had been charged and I had been in the jail and that. I got emotional, ken, because the judge had said – you'll no' be going back on another picket line. That was conditions of bail.

I didnae say I wasnae going back tae the strike centre but I said I wouldnae go picketing again and that was hurting me. But after speaking tae my wife we decided that I wouldnae go that way, I would still go picketing and if I got the jail then so be it. But that was the only hard time because I had never been in the jail, I had never been in trouble before and at that particular time I did get emotional. In saying that I wouldnae have gi'en it up for a' the world. I can always look back on it now and say – I did that, I did this. I did it because I thought it was right.

My daughters, they were just kids like, but they kent I was in the jail. I mean, I'm no' afraid tae tell anybody, I'm quite proud about it now because, at the end o' the day, as far as I was concerned, I was fighting for my job. I was fighting for a' the pits. It was harder for a lot o' guys but I was fortunate in the fact that my wife backed me up. And if the strike did anything for us, it brought us closer thegether. I must say that. We have a marriage like everybody else, we fa' out and we fa' in, but through that period my wife backed me tae the hilt.

If I was tae get up at seven o'clock in the morning tae go picketing and no' come hame tae seven o'clock at night, she accepted that. And we just made dae. We didnae hae any money. We had each other, we had the kids. But we were feeding ourselves and that was it, ken.

It changed my views. It made me more politically aware o' what was going on in the country. Before, I couldnae tell you what was going on but, after the strike, I joined the Labour Party. I'm in the local Labour Party in the village. I was elected, at a mass meeting tae become the delegate for SCEBTA at the colliery. Our delegate had been sacked because him and the NUM delegate went and sat down the pit, a sit-in, and they never got their jobs back. I was elected in the interim, hoping he would get his job back, but he never did and I've been the delegate since.

Getting more intae the union, seeing what went on, going tae conferences and things like that, I became more politically aware o' my surroundings. I tried tae influence my wife and my lassies and the rest o' the members o' my family. I read a' the papers that's going if I can get them. I like the news on the television although it doesnae always tell you the truth. That's what the strike did for me; it made me more politically aware of what's going on, no' just in Britain, but the world, about apartheid, about what's going on in Israel, a' those things that before I wasnae even interested in.

Nuclear disarmament. Before, you could have had a million nuclear submarines and a million nuclear bombs, tae me it didnae matter; but now it does matter tae me.

We didnae get as much support in the village as we deserved, I must say that, but the support we did get was generous, to say the least. I think a lot o' people in the village who didnae know me before, know me now. It was like a lot o' other villages, we had our ups and downs and we did have our arguments, no doubt about it, but we just had tae sort them out. But the village itself was affected by the strike because, as I said, Kelty was brought up on mining and there was six or seven pits here at one time.

During the strike we were united throughout the country bar the boys in Nottingham. It just seemed tae be a common fight for everybody. And now, when you look, the years have come on now and we're into 1994, things have changed. I don't think now, that you'll ever change anything with a mass picket. I was up at Dundee, at Timex, it was a big picket. As long as the legislation's there to hold you back I don't think you'll get anywhere. I think the days of mass picketing are past.

Looking at us and the National Area now, I think we've went too far down the road. There's no' a lot o' us left and what I think our grievance is, is that Arthur still seems to be hell-bent on action, action, action and I don't think he realises how much men have got to lose. In some of the pits now, no' them a', but some o' them, a lot o' the men can make good money and they're just no' prepared tae go down the line o' going on strike after strike after strike and continuing tae lose money.

A lot o' them now are ten years older, a lot o' them have got families and they're no' prepared tae put their jobs on the line because they've got mortgages and cars. They're only wanting a normal way of living same as everybody else. Fae what we see up here, and I'm no' saying we're always right, by the way, there doesnae seem to be anything going on. There's nae talk on wages, there's nae talk on safety. In fact they're no' talking wi' anybody on anything at a' tae dae wi' conditions at the pit and tae me, that's no' how we should be going.

As a delegate my first job at the pit is tae ensure that the men have got good conditions, good wages and everything else appertaining tae that and I don't think the National Area's daein that. I'm no' saying Scotland's always right, we're no' always right, but that's the things I see. From then when we were a' thegether and now. There's a thing there I brought up fae the club, the *Yorkshire Miner* I think it's called, saying the pits were united on that first day of action and that's no' true.

I saw a fax that was delivered tae our pit after the second day of action and there was over fifteen, maybe twenty, pits working. Now I'm no' saying they're scabs, I'm no' saying anything like that, but that's how dis-united we are. We're no' united, we're dis-united. I got shown that at first hand in 1991. I had the pleasure tae represent the Scottish Area at Blackpool at the National Conference, and when we went tae the rostrum they booed and they hissed us.

Now, Nicky Wilson was talking on safety, and for anybody tae boo a person talking on safety or rebuke a person talking on safety tae me is all wrong because that particular year we had something like nine men killed in the industry.

I'm no' asking Arthur Scargill tae go and talk tae the UDM, because I hate them as much as anybody, but if he's tae go intae a room and sit across the table, or up the other end o' the table fae whoever it is and talk tae British Coal about my wages and my conditions, that's what I want him tae dae.

I cannae see much o' a future for the mining industry as long as the Tory Government's there. I think if the Labour Party had got in then we would be looking forward tae a good future. I would like tae see an energy policy for Britain wi' coal as the base. I'm no' saying we should dae away wi' nuclear or oil or gas or anything like that but, because coal is in abundance, make coal the base and then start fae there. Keep the pits that we've got, try and keep the pits that we've got, dinnae let them go down below what we've got suppose we've tae inject money into them.

I cannae see the mining industry coming up tae be the force that it was years and years ago. But I'd like tae think that we'll go intae the next century and that someday, sometime, somehow, we'll get our heads together and start tae talk tae British Coal.

My father and my grandfather and a' them were in the mining industry and I would hate tae think what they would think now if they were here, if they were alive, and seen what's happened tae the mining industry.

There is a big problem in Kelty with unemployment, but saying that, a lot o' guys that went out the pit got jobs in the dockyard, were lucky enough tae get jobs in the dockyard and different places. For instance, my brother, he works wi' the council as a road sweeper, x amount o' guys in Kelty got jobs in the dockyard. Although there was an unemployment problem, it wasnae any greater than it's been for a long time. The biggest employer is the dockyard, quite a lot still work in the pit, a' the rest work at other things or dinnae work at a'.

The walk* for me was a fantastic experience. We suffered a lot o' aches and pains but throughout the country everybody just wanted tae see you. Folk wanted tae touch us. Everywhere we went we got a great reception, even in Tory towns and Tory councils. As we went on and on, further down the road, it got easier and easier and the police were good tae us.

* Reference to the march by a group of Scottish miners to London following the pit closure announcements by the government in 1992.

I was in places I never thought I would ever visit. Some nights we slept in nice hotels, other nights we slept in sleeping bags in church halls. Looking back, the walk was a great thing. Again, it's a thing you can always look yourself in the mirror and say I did it, I was there. I remember one day we were coming into Maltby and we saw a car in the distance. And as we got nearer somebody said, that's Tommy Brennan, who used tae be convener at Ravenscraig. He had a table laid out on the road and he had cans o' beer on it and miniature bottles o' House of Commons whisky.

The policemen who had been wi' us at that particular time had been good tae us, they looked after us. When we got tae Maltby we still had the miniatures in our pockets and we decided tae give them to the police. They came up tae us and told us they had tae go, this was their patch finished. One of them came up and I shook hands wi' him and said there's a wee present for you. It was a great experience.

BILLY MCLEAN

Kelty

I started in the pit in February 1960, which is more than thirty years ago and I've seen a hell of a lot o' changes. When I started in the pit, oh my God, everybody was miners, like. I was brought up in Lumphinnans which was a real mining community at that time when I was a laddie.

It was known as Little Moscow at that time and I was brought up in the mining union tradition, we were a' sort o' communistic-minded in Lumphinnans when I was a laddie. When I was young I was communistic-minded but as you get older that changes, I suppose.

I started in the Alice Pit in 1960. I left there and went to

Westthorpe Colliery where I met my wife and got married and I came back to Bogside Mine. That was when the wages struggle in the late 1960s started when we wernae getting the wages that we should have been getting. 1971, I believe, was the first sort o' national strike that we had. That lasted about three weeks, unofficial. I could be wrong, it could have been '69. Anyway I went away to England then. I started in Shirebrook Colliery near Mansfield. I was there during the 1972 strike. I actually was on the picket lines at Saltley when we closed the gates that day – it was a turning point in the strike.

After the strike I came back tae Scotland tae work in Solsgirth and I was there during the 1974 strike which was a walkover for us. During those days we were a very powerful union, no doubt about that, and as the years went by were were daein a'right and then in 1977 we'd a ballot about whether we wanted an incentive scheme or no', which a lot, in fact the majority, of the men were against.

And, by the way, we were on strike during Christmas tae get an incentive scheme because in Solsgirth we were producing an awful lot o' coal at that time and, thinking back, maybe we were wrong going for an incentive scheme, but in saying that, that was the way we felt at that time.

Thinking back, that was the beginning o' the end for us, wi' the incentive scheme, because we started what they said would happen: pit against pit, men against men and everything. A lot o' men wouldnae agree wi' that but I think it was one of our downfalls, the incentive scheme.

Obviously the Tories had been preparing tae take the miners on, as far as I'm concerned, as revenge for '74. I was always militant, I never crossed a picket line, I was always very militant. I voted for strike action, for industrial action, everything like that.

And then in 1981 we decided tae come out, the strike lasted a week then they came on the television and said it was all over they were going tae invest in the pits. At that time you didnae realise what the Tories were at because, obviously, they had set their tactics doon, they hadnae everything in place at that particular time.

So, by the time 1984 came they must have been ready for us because they decided tae shut Cortonwood Colliery and, of course, being the Yorkshire miners, a wee bit hasty, they came oot on strike and everybody else came oot on strike. Being a militant, myself, or being a militant-minded person at that particular time, I thought that the rest o' the miners would just respect the picket line.

But when it come tae the crunch, what we should have expected from the Nottingham miners happened, because in 1971 and 1972 thé Nottinghamshire miners area didnae gie us a vote for strike action. They were always reluctant for strike action so we should have been prepared for that, and we werenae. Anyway the Nottinghamshire miners had their own ballot and decided tae go their own way.

Well, I thought – scabs, scabs, scabs, and at that time I believed in the principle that you shouldnae cross a picket line. I was on strike for a year, we had a hard time o' it for two years, I got arrested twice. I could've lost my job; it could have been a lot worse for me. It was bad enough as it was, sheriff officers at my door and a' the rest o' it, but I would never scab, never scab, never cross a picket line.

But unfortunately there were miners who wanted to cross the picket lines and obviously we werenae going to get the support o' the rest o' the trade union movement while they men were working.

Anyway, after the strike we got back and me personally I had always been dayshift or piece-time shift – that's starting ten o'clock in the morning or seven o'clock in the morning. So, anyway, they left me and my team for two or three weeks and then a' of a sudden we got a line – constant nightshift. So I thought, aw they're fucking at it, ken, this is no real. I hadnae done nightshift for, God Almighty, for a lot o' years.

I went tae see the deputy manager who I had had a run in wi' before, like. I says, look sir, I'm prepared tae go three shifts, my neighbours they're prepared tae go three shifts but we're no' accepting constant nightshift. This is only three weeks after the strike, by the way.

He says, look, you and your neighbours are constant nightshift. He says, if you're no' happy wi' the job and, by the way, it's your job and you're staying on it, there's nae three shifts for you there's nae nothing for you, it's constant nightshift or there's the fucking gate.

So then I was beat. After the strike we were a' beat. It was a bad time for us after being so strong, like, in years gaun back. So anyway, I accepted and I was constant nightshift for something like ten weeks before, fortunately for me, we got a new deputy manager. I knew the guy fae a few years back and it changed a wee bit and I managed tae get back tae the shifts we had been on before.

But, looking back on it, my ain view on it is that we were really up against it, the Tories, like. But I will say this, if the miners had've had a ballot, and a lot o' miners will say this tae you, we could have outvoted the Nottinghamshire miners. We could have got the vote for strike action and we would have got it nae bother because by this time we only needed fifty-one per cent o' the vote. If we had done that as early in 1984 as May we would have won it and the Nottinghamshire miners would have had to stick to it.

But Arthur Scargill, being the man that he is, thought that every miner would respect the picket lines and it never happened. It just didnae happen. Looking back, we made some hell of a mistakes as a union. But when you're in a situation like that and you think, well we won in '74, we won in '72, we could dae it again, if we're united we could win again. But we werenae at the end o' the day and there were a lot o' things that went wrong that should never have happened.

At that time I was very bitter, especially after the strike; I was very bitter. Very bitter. But I realised I had tae get on wi' things, like. And we had a bad time o' it, after it. But, life goes on and you've just got tae pick things up and start again and that's what most o' the boys had tae dae.

I'm still in the pit, but I'm in the process o' coming oot now because I've had enough, like. I've done thirty-three years and I'm no' as fit as I used tae be and I'm just ready for coming out. Just ready for jacking in.

The miners' strike personally at times was very, very hard but other times it was very, very good because o' the comradeship. In Kelty itself the comradeship and the support o' the Kelty people was great.

I think if I had lived elsewhere, If I had been living in Mansfield where I was working in Shirebrook, in that particular area on the borderline o' the scabs in Nottinghamshire and the guys in Derbyshire and Yorkshire that were oot on strike I think it would have been a hell of a lot harder.

Looking back, I can remember going tae Florence Colliery as early as May during the strike and I couldnae believe it. There were scabs going in on the nightshift and we stayed there tae picket the dayshift and they were drawing up in double decker buses, and the double decker buses were fu'. A lot o' us should ha' kent at that time it was going to be an uphill battle but we thought we could still possible win.

I was younger then. It's alright tae say after the event what you would dae, but when you're in the position what dae you dae? If a guy comes tae the house and says what are you going tae dae, are you gaunnae sit in the house or are you gaunnae go on the picket lines, what dae you dae? You're gaunnae go out on the picket lines.

Some o' the things I did during the strike I wouldnae dae again. The police were just as bad as the scabs. You went to a pit and you knew their starting time was seven o'clock in the morning and you'd be there fae half-past five in the morning and the police, in my opinion, deliberately kept the scabs back tae as late a nine o'clock in the morning. And you're standing there for three and a half hours. That was a wee bit heart-breaking, morale-wise it wasnae very good.

We had one scab in Kelty and they used tae send mair than a dozen policemen, in fact I'm sure one particular morning there must have been about twenty o' them just tae get one man tae his work. The cost must have been phenomenal. There's naebody'll ever know the true cost o' the miners' strike. The truth o' the matter is that the Tories wanted revenge for the Seventies, Maggie Thatcher and her cronies and people in the back room, the high financiers, people whose names we'll never know. We know McGregor was a hatchet man sent in. At the end o' the day it wasnae just solely about pit closures or economics.

How could it be about economics or pit closures? It was simply that the trade union movement and us the miners that had beat a Tory government had tae be beat so that they could set about the rest o' the British trade union movement tae finish off wi' the situation we've got the day, like the Timex situation. A lot o' people will say it's a lot o' rubbish but it's no', because it a' stemmed fae beating the miners.

It's history now. What we got is what's going on today: people working for £2.50 an hour when they should be working for at least £4.50 an hour. That's my opinion, by the way.

I've got my regrets that I spent thirty-three years in the pits, especially after the strike, after the last few years when I've seen what they've done to us, the slaughter that's went on o' the miners. I've often wished that when I was young I had been a joiner or a plumber or something else like that. But then again I think I've been a miner, I've been through the struggle, I've seen thirty-three years of struggle, like, fae I was a laddie in the pits.

And the changes in the pits. I've went fae pits wi' five and six hundred men in them that produced 2,000 tonnes o' coal a week tae a situation where I was going intae sections wi' another nine or ten men and producing about 2,000 tonne of coal in one shift, in six hours and before that it was taking 600 men a week when I was a laddie tae produce the same amount o' coal. So the changes I've seen have been absolutely fantastic.

The management we had before the strike, you could argue wi' them and negotiate wi' them, you could get concessions and various other things. After the strike you couldnae dae that. They hammered doon on everything. The argument was that the management had the right tae manage and that there was nobody else going tae manage the pit, there was naebody else gaun tae dae anything and it was a simple as that.

At Castlebridge it did change because I think management realised they had tae get back a wee bit better relationship tae get the manpower and everything, tae get the coal out. I will say that at Castlebridge at the present time the management isnae too bad. They can be hard when they want tae be hard but they are quite reasonable.

It's still no' the same, I don't think it'll ever be the same but it did get back tae a bit better than what it was. I'm ready to come out when I get the chance, definitely.

The stories I could tell. I mind when I was on the Saltley picket line I lost one o' my shoes. And we were on a surge forward, we were up against the police and everything and I was in there wi' wan shoe. And I'm saying, that's me beat noo, I've lost my bloody shoe. And then we went back again and all of a sudden an arm goes up, it was my shoe, like. That was the kind o' time it was. There was none o' the brutality in '72 wi' the police as there was in '84.

The Orgreave picket line was unbelievable. The tactics in Scotland were to stop the pickets fae gaun where they wanted tae go. At Orgreave they said we'll no' stop them getting. Another thing was that they wouldnae let you intae Nottinghamshire, it was cocooned. We tried it and we couldnae get in. At Orgreave it was nae problem, you never seen a policeman, right in, in you go. The only reason they let us in was because they knew we were a' there. It was like a battlefield.

They let us in so they could keep us there and they could get us there. I didnae agree wi' some o' the younger boys throwing stones, the marshalling should have been a wee bit better. There were missiles thrown at the police but I still don't think it was an excuse for what they did after that.

After the first push they broke ranks and the next thing you ken they came through on horseback wi' batons this bloody length and when they were let loose that was it. They were only intent in battering hell out o' the miners after that. And they did. They battered fuck oot o' us a' day. If the boys on the horses missed you they had the boys wi' the wee batons cleaning up at the back. Then they would retreat.

A lot o' the young boys on the picket line, and by the way it was a joke, it wasnae a picket line after that, they were a' running about wi' their t-shirts and their training shoes and their jeans, nae weapons o' any description, and they were chasing up against the police. Of course the police were coming back wi' their batons and everything and they were knocking fuck oot o' them. It was a no-win situation.

Our group decided that this was no longer a picket line, it was a battleground, if we stayed we were just going tae get battered by the police. We decided tae leave. It was a red hot day and most o' us were ready for a pint o' beer. We got into this club and *News at One* comes on. And what we seen on the television was completely different tae what we had actually experienced. We had only left a mile away and we'd been through it and we'd seen it and we'd been there and what we saw on the television was, tae us, completely different. It just wasnae the true facts. It was unreal. You've got tae experience it tae believe it.

Looking back I don't suppose I would dae the same again. I wouldnae go through the same again. Naebody in their right mind would go through the same again. If you were told what you were going tae come up against for a year, what you were going tae be forced intae, what was going tae happen tae you and everything, you wouldnae dae it.

For a long time I was bitter, but it's in the past noo. I'll never forgive the scabs, never. I was down in Cowdenbeath the other day and I saw one and the first thing that hits your mind when you look at them is – scab. You cannae help it. When you've been through what most o' the miners have been through, how dae they expect us tae feel.

I would never have believed that we would have been reduced tae where we are noo. Never have believed it. The trade unions are too weak noo because they've got every man looking over their shoulders saying, when's my turn next, when am I going tae lose my job. If Margaret Thatcher achieved one thing, she achieved that.

ARCHIE CAMPBELL

Kelty

I'm sixty-nine years of age. There were seven or eight pits in the village at one time and I worked in, I would say, six o' them. I never got sacked once. I sacked myself often enough under privatisation.

Since privatisation I felt that the pits were far happier places to work in and you got a better crack o' the whip, a fairer deal until they started pit closures. I took an active part against pit closures in the early '50s and '60s. It didnae dae much good eventually. Even under a Labour government they closed mair pits or every bit as many as Mrs Thatcher has closed.

Thinking back, our leadership wasnae as good as we thought they were. We followed them blindly and I could condemn them for accepting paltry 1/6 and three bob a week or a day on your wages. They talk about miners getting a fortune? No way, when you hear what they're getting out o' a dockyard. I remember when I was a boy at the school we always said that the dockyard was a convalescent home for the lame, the sick and the lazy. Mind you, they didnae get well paid but they didnae dae very much work either.

The '72 and '74 strikes were hard, but we won and, I'll tell you, we won handsomely. Tae think we had tae wait a' that time tae get a decent rise on our wages.

Mrs Thatcher prepared very well for the '84 strike. Myself, I had replacement knee joints and if you could cry me lucky I was one of the lucky boys, I was on the insurance during the '84 strike. Wi' my experience o' the '72 and '74 strikes I went out o' my way tae assist the young lads, organised the strike committee and things like that.

Once things got started and I thought they were gaun in the right direction I bowed out because the fact that I was on insurance during a' that period made me feel that I wasnae entitled tae shout the odds as militantly as I would have had I been completely well because I'm a boy that likes tae open my big gub back and forward and I felt that I wasnae entitled tae try and influence the boys who were getting bugger-all when I was getting insurance.

I was also lucky that my wife was working tae so, frankly, the '84 strike was nae hardship as far as I was concerned. Fortunately, by that time, my family were a' working. They gied their mother the dig money on the Friday but they mooched it back on the Saturday morning when I was awa' doon the pub.

I took an active part in the picketing and things like that and I found that the police didnae gie us a fair crack o' the whip where we were in the minority. We got the boot laid intae us where we were in the minority but if we outnumbered them they were the most helpful people you could wish tae talk tae.

I used tae have a lot o' respect and I still do think policemen are needed but I often say tae myself, where did they a' go after the '84 strike? There were millions o' them. We've got a village here and we used tae hae a sergeant and six policemen here resident. I think you've tae phone Whitehall 1212 tae get a policeman in Kelty now.

I saw things that turned my stomach. I wouldnae like our boys ever tae go through the likes o' that again; it was a long bloody time tae go without a piece and living on handouts and things like that. They were magnificent, the boys. You always got one that wanted tae upset the applecart but they were dealt wi' in a manner befitting.

I saw hardship. But I saw where some o' our boys in the pit, if they were working in the city, they would be millionaires because they would get a living out o' bugger-all.

It's no' the same village. The attitude o' what miners is left in the village is that they say being in the pits noo is like being in the Bar-L, you're feared tae open your gub. At one time you could argue the toss wi' an official and discuss things but now it's – you dae it or get your jacket on, simple as that. Just like back tae privatisation. I worked nine years under privatisation and they were the worst nine years I ever worked in the pit because you never had a leg tae stand on. I've never been back tae the pit since the strike, but talking tae the young boys, they say it's hellish.

If I had my life tae live again there would be nae pits for me. When I see what I got in the pit and what I come out the pit wi'.

There's been changes, but no' for the good. People are no' as closely knit as they were before.

THE LOTHIANS

ANDREW LEYS

Whitburn

I left school and had one job before I started in the pit, it was at Arthur Engineering, a wee firm down in Bathgate as an apprentice turner. I did six months of that, paid an absolute pittance, a tenner a week. Fiver to my Mo', fiver to myself, and I tapped about three, four pound off her during the week.

So I put in for the pit. That was the year the miners were on strike and they had the power cuts. I started then, just after the strike. I was interviewed and taken on and my wages more than doubled, so I was quite happy. I never went back to any sort of trade or anything like that.

I was always meaning to go back to school. Well, I did a certain amount of time at college doing a deputy's course, but they were telling us nothing new, you wernae learning anything. The first six months I learned absolutely nothing, so I left that.

'At the time, when I started in the pit, the wages were good, for me anyway. Then going through the years, I got married. The weans never came about till after the strike anyway. But all the lead up, I did all the oncost jobs, all the outby jobs and then you went to the face at eighteen/nineteen.

We're talking in 1993 the now, and the same things are happening in '93 as happened then. The threat of your job going, nobody likes that. Well, we've gone through it and we didnae like it and I just feel so sorry for the boys that are going to be going through it. Because the chances of jobs are minimum. I'm quite lucky the now, like, being in employment but . . .

The principle [of the strike] remains the same, trying to protect jobs. Especially when you've got a resource that's down there that you can never go back to. They'll never be able to re-open Bilston Glen, they'll no' be able to re-open Polkemmet or any of the pits that have shut since then. And it is a national asset and I think it's a waste, no' just of the miners' resources and skills that the miners had to get the coal out, no' just talking about miners as a whole but o' everybody that was involved in a pit from the canteen woman to the boy that was operating the shearer. It's just a waste o' a' their resources, for the nation.

We are for better or worse, even though there are a lot of us Scottish nationalists or something like that, we're on an island. We have got an island mentality, whether we want it or no'. But we're no' taking care o' this island. Never done it back in 1984/'85 and we're no' doing it now.

Well, we went through that year. There's a lot of things done and said at that time you thought were right. But wi' a lot o' hindsight and wi' a lot o' years under your belt, your views change. I think, when they came out with the closures, with hindsight, if they had have organised a national ballot, I think there would have been the support there wi' the miners for strike action, whatever means were deemed necessary to stop them going through. It would have swung in favour of trying to stop it instead o' lying back and letting everybody trample o'er the top of us. The history of the British working class eh?

There would have been the support there, because there was great public support as well. And if the ballot had came about it would have legitimated the action that the miners were taking. And it would have staved off the criticism and possibly led to more support from the public or whoever.

The violence that went on in the strike, I think, you could never support, ken, some o' the actions. That boy that was killed down in Wales, crazy. But the thing they were living with, it changed a lot of people. The circumstances – I'm no' saying they drove them to it, but there was a sense o' unlawfulness about a lot of things during that time. A lot of the miners thought they could take the law into their own hands, where we know we cannae.

We've all got certain rules and regulations, you just cannae go beyond them, or you shouldnae anyway.

The strike was a great laugh, like, a brilliant laugh. We had some funny times, down South, about this area as well. It's all the wee characters that you met, they were on a different planet.

Polkemmet was a big body blow. The union, for right or wrong reasons, gave the management the opportunity to flood the pit, which we should never have done. You should always give cover at all times. Even the boys that might be facing a strike the now, they should always give the cover and maintain the fabric o' their industry. We're there to work and those boys want the pits now the way we wanted them then. Never give anybody the opportunity to take away your jobs because that's the crisis that they're in.

During the strike we knew it was shut and after we went back we got shipped through to Bilston Glen which was a different ball game all together. A lot o' bitterness through there. A lot o' resentment. You could feel it. We were known as hardliners and I think the boys from Polkemmet introduced a different sort of atmosphere into the place because we wernae taking the nonsense a lot of the managers had in their heads through there. I think that's where a lot of the disputes started, wi' boys from Polkemmet at Bilston Glen.

The management were very unreasonable through there. But there were some great characters through in Bilston and they are the guys you remember the most. At Polkemmet, you had a lot of characters, they were all older boys. We were, what, twenty year-old, twenty to thirty, and they used to keep in their own sort of clique. But when you went through there the age difference wasnae that great. It was a young workforce.

When we went through from Polkemmet to Bilston Glen, and I think a lot of the boys will agree with me, it was constant harassment from the managers. No' just to the NUM men, you got it going towards the NACODS men as well. And they are classed in British management structure as middle management, and they were hassled to death, as much as we were and possibly even more. And you had some good blokes in NACODS. We had one or two good gaffers.

There was masses of investment in Bilston Glen but it always seemed to go wrong. They never seemed to have any plan. They never salvaged anything out there. It was all wrong. A lot of that equipment could have been re-used. Some of the maintenance programmes were terrible as well, ken, just run it till it blows up.

When the pit shut I got my interview first thing in the morning and, like we all did, took the money and ran. I wasnae glad to leave it, but I wasnae sad to leave it, sort of thing, because at that time everybody had had so bloody much. I was out looking for work that day. I went into Livingston, into the industrial estates, got a pile of application forms.

I was on lieu of notice for twelve weeks, so we had money in our pockets. I bought a brand new bike. It's still lying out in the garage. It gets an airing every year, like.

It was as bad then as it is now. If employment prospects were nil then they must be minus something now. I wasny working for about two months then I got a job and stayed for a couple of years. It was a good enough job but with personality conflicts and one thing and another I packed it in, about two weeks before Christmas in 1991. Crazy, eh?

Then I started on the taxis full time, which is a terrible job. But it paid the rent and you canny complain because I've got commitments now that I never had during the miners' strike. I never had weans at that time. The commitments are different now because you have to put shoes on weans' feet and at the end of the day you have to bring money in. Money's no' everything, but it helps a hell of a lot, like.

So I was on the taxis for about six months or so and I got an opportunity to get into a Japanese company in Livingston, which I'm now at, very happily. As opposed to the pits, it's a non-union plant. But you don't have the need for a union as much. The management are no' the same way. They're no' vindictive, they're no' petty in the way most miners experienced, post-strike. I like it. Pays the rent as well. They treat you well if you show a wee bit of initiative, no' like the pit. There, if you showed a wee bit of initiative, they put you on a belt switch out the road. Far too smart, get rid o' him. But out there if you show a wee bit of initiative they nurture it.

Out here we've got Levis in Whitburn. Apart from Levis, the Cameron Iron Works. In this area, in West Lothian as a whole, if it wasnae for the inward investment from foreign companies in Livingston, God knows what it would be like. It would be brutal.

The strike was an experience. I dinnae regret anything I've done in my life, if things happen they happen. If it had been handled differently possibly it could have been better, the prospects for people in the country could have been better, for me, for the kids, I don't know. But the things that have happened have happened and it's all history now.

The experience of the strike stood everybody in good stead. You don't panic. We never starved then and we'll no' starve now. It makes you appreciate people a lot more as well. It makes you appreciate work a hell of a lot more, because that wee spell I was unemployed for, God almighty, nobody could survive on state benefits. You need a job to keep you going.

Some boys have never worked since Polkemmet. Older guys really, ones who were hitting forty odds even at that time, in 1984, and that's sad because those boys had a lot to offer as well. They talk about market forces, but they could create jobs, real jobs because the fabric of society is falling down about our ears, the state of the housing, the state of the roads.

Things are just different now, they're so bloody, radically different. Look at the eighties, the boom years that are coming back to haunt everybody in Britain. Everybody's bloody terrified to even buy a new television set. It's no' right that people should be so afraid for their jobs. If, God forbid, I was put out of work tomorrow, what would my prospects be? They would be the same as what they were, even worse, than in 1988, 'cause there's nothing here. This country's a mess.

I know a guy who's been left school for twenty-three years and never had a job, he doesnae want a job. Now, he's one o' that minority. But I ken a lot o' boys who desperately want to work. And it doesnae matter to them what they're doing. Shovel shit for a full day. Doesnae matter. As long as you can support the people that are important to you.

It really opens your eyes when you're made redundant. We were in wee safe jobs until we got put out of work. Things do change and it makes you realise that it is hard. Because in the pit you did have a fairly good standard of living, you had your job, whether you enjoyed it or no' was up to the individual. But at the end of the day, when you get out into that big hard world out there, it's a hell o' a lot different. It makes you appreciate a lot more things.

My prospects look good now, to me they look good. I'm with a company that hopefully I can get on in and I hope to be there until I draw my pension. That's the big thing in most folk's minds now, security.

MICK McGAHEY

Penicuik

I was born in Glasgow and moved through to Edinburgh in 1967/'68, left the school at fifteen, went to Bilston Glen and started working in April, fifth o' April 1971, and worked there for thirteen years, eight months until I was sacked during the miners' strike.

The strike itself, ken, I mean it was something that couldnae be avoided. In 1981, you had something like 150,000 miners going on strike and it lasted three or four days and it was about closure and things like that, about a number o' issues. But the one thing about that is Thatcher was cute enough to stand back fae the thing and say 'Well, I'm no' ready yet.'

At that time you didnae realise that Ridley was drawing up his programme on how to defeat the miners with the transport and the shipping o' coal and the importation o' coal, all that kind of thing.

We thought in 1981, or most people who were actively involved at that time, that Thatcher was backing down, but she wasnae backing down, she was standing back and planning up her strategy. And she was picking her time.

And to a certain degree when the '84 strike started, it wasnae started because of the union, it was started because o' the government. They had picked their time. They had decided this was the time to fight.

They wanted to fight in March and they wanted it at that particular time so it would go through the summer and everybody knew that. We a' knew it wasnae the right time to fight but when your back's to the wa' that was it, you had to fight. And the one thing that the leadership knew then, once we overcame the initial problems that they would have wi' getting the miners on strike, they knew they would get a solid response. And that was what they got.

The strike itself was, I think, for about the first nine months, something that a lot o' people were proud to be on. To be a miner and to be on strike. Until such times as you had people drifting back.

I had always attended branch meetings, until I was about eighteen/nineteen but never been involved as a committee member or anything like that.

I was elected onto the committee the November/December prior to the strike. So I was only on the committee about four months before the strike started, which was good for me as an education, because obviously when we realised the strike was going to take place there was a great deal o' planning went on, making sure we got a result and that we didnae get egg on our face.

So there was a lot o' meetings took place, particularly within the Left where we worked out strategy, what we were gonnae dae. And to a certain degree it was effective everywhere. The only problem we had in Scotland, I would say, would be Bilston Glen, my own pit. And that lasted for three days and that was it then resolved. And it was done through traditional tactics – picketing.

The start of the strike was quite a traumatic time but it was interesting, it was good. The thing that stands out is the solidarity, particularly the first six months wi' all the workers that were involved, the miners that were involved, the people that were involved and the solidarity that came from other trade unions, particularly SOGAT. No' just the money but the practical things that they gave to strike centres like foodstuffs, but also toiletries and stuff like that that women would use.

It wasnae just about men being on strike, it was about women and men and their families and a lot of the unions reflected that in the type of stuff that they gave and in the way that they gave it.

The one thing that happened was that I got arrested nine times during the strike, well it was five times and nine charges, and out of that it was four I was convicted o' and five I wasnae. I think that the thing that stands out is that the Coal Board could just sack you for committing a criminal offence, or what was recognised as a criminal offence, which was relatively nothing to do with the actual pit itself.

You were sacked, no' on the basis o' your work record, but because they used the arrests politically just to get rid o' you; because they saw you as an undesirable. And that in itself you expect. If you're involved politically then you expect that kind of thing to happen, there's nothing new in it. It happened in 1926. It happened to my grandfather in 1926 and it's happened to thousands and thousands o' other workers prior to that and up to now.

Take a look at Timex this last few months. They're tried and tested tactics that an employer always uses whether it's a nationalised industry or a private concern.

At that particular time it didnae have that much effect getting the sack. To a certain degree it was like earning your stripes, you know. You were seen to be doing the business, you know, on the picket lines and stuff like that. At that time nobody really thought that the strike would go for a year. We thought that everything would be sorted out after the strike, everything would be hunky-dory. At that particular time we didn't realise that there was the actual political change taking place within the Coal Board.

We did pit head collections every Friday and the main problem was that, at the end o' the strike, you started off wi' thirty or forty people standing outside Bilston Glen and various other pits, but by the second year it was only two or three. It was after the first six months, though, that it really started to affect people. People really realised that they wernae going to take you back.

The strike ended in the March and the union managed to get a review o' our cases where we went and got interviewed, in my case by the manager, and it was just a farce. They had nae intentions of ever taking certain individuals back. They had already made up their minds to make a token effort and take back one or two people and that's what they did. But they actually put people in a position where they raised their hopes about getting their jobs back and just dumped them again. And that was done twice.

But right up until the time where Bilston Glen was shut, and that was a few years after the strike, my intentions were that I was going back working in the pit. But when Bilston Glen was shut that was the bubble burst for me. There was no longer a pit there to go back to so I decided that I would do something else.

Up until that time I had tried to find work and after hundreds and hundreds of applications a' I got was a job training scheme, putting up fences and building dry stane dyke walls. I enjoyed it, it was alright, twenty-four hours over three days a week. We were living off that and we were living off the compensation we got from the tribunals system. So, financially we lived well, reasonably well; certainly no worse off than what we would have been if we were still in the pit.

But the realisation that you couldnae get employment, that you had become unemployable was a bit o' a shock. Myself, I mean, I was always taught to take pride in what I'm doing. The boss isnae the one who makes the wheels go round, it's the worker. And I was proud to work in a pit. It was a proud place to work. It took a couple o' years to realise I wasnae getting any jobs back there.

November '86 to November '87 I was on the Job Creation, and the reason I did that was because I had got money from the industrial tribunal and therefore I wasnae getting any social security. So the only alternative I had was to live off the £8,500 compensation or to add to that by taking on Job Creation.

So that was what I did. I enjoyed it: it got me fit again. I was climbing up and down hills with bags o' trees and spades and hammers and stuff like that. And the people I was working with were all youngsters, eighteen and nineteen, some of them twenty-one and twenty-two, who had never had a real job before. It gave me a sort of insight into how other people have had to live. I had been sheltered through having a job leaving school at fifteen up until the strike and it was a full sort of life.

After the pit shut I thought, well, that's the end of it, like. As far as the pit's concerned we wernae going to get a job. We had had all these promises from the Labour Party and from Neil Kinnock that if Labour got power then the victimised miners would be reinstated. The problem was that that wasnae going to be the case because Labour couldnae get power through their own incompetence.

That year that I had worked on the community programme I hadnae really tried that much to get a job because an election was due and all the rest of it. So, after that, I just started writing away again to different places and I wrote to Lothian Health Board.

I actually wrote to all the hospitals and I think what happened was that the Health Board personnel department was at the Astley Ainslie and my letters kept going to them so somebody in that office must have had a look at them and said well, this guy's looking for a job because they got about ten letters from me all saying the same thing, and they offered me a job.

So, I went for the interview with the head porter and the administrator and explained why I couldnae give them references. I told them that I had worked on a community programme and under the circumstances, considering that I had won an industrial tribunal, you know, they took a reference from the community programme manager and I started the following week and I've worked there for five years come October.

The consequences of the last ten years? I mean, relatively speaking, I've came out unscathed. Leading up to the strike, during the strike and after the strike I had the support of my wife so I didn't have a problem in terms of the family. It didnae really affect my health.

There's a lot of men who suffered severe depression because they couldnae find work. I seemed to bounce through that without any problem. I had one period for about two weeks where I felt really depressed and felt I had to go and see the doctor about it. But it only lasted for about two weeks and then that was me bounced back again.

I've enjoyed the last ten years. The year of the strike was probably one of the best years of my life. I went all over the place. I met a lot of people I knew because of my father and I met a lot of new people and I made a lot of good friends and most of them still are.

The initial mothballing of Monktonhall and the closure of Bilston Glen had a traumatic effect on this area. In the street I stay in here right now, when Bilston Glen was in its heyday, eighty per cent of the people who lived in the houses in this street all worked in the pits – worked in Bilston Glen. Now there's one guy works at Castlebridge and that's the sole contribution to the mining industry in this street whereas before that about eighty families earned their livelihood. And that's no' just eighty individuals, that's eighty fathers wi' two or three sons working in the industry.

All the small supply industries collapsed. There are very few engineering factories left. Coal companies, in terms of jobs for coal porters, that's all went to the wall. It's had an effect.

At it stands now the area's got nothing for kids. There are kids in this street now who are of employment age and they've never had jobs and they'll probably no' get jobs. I would have been happy for my son to work in Bilston Glen, along wi' me.

My daughter, the way it's going, she'll no' find any real employment, because there isnae any factories, there isnae any skilled workplaces round about this area. There's no' any industrial base in this area now. There's no base for any jobs. Certainly I would have been happy to see my son working in the pit. I think now I would push more for them to take up further education, to seek employment in areas I would normally not have tried to influence them going into.

The one thing that I did notice when I started working in the hospital is that the sense of solidarity amongst different workers wasnae there. What has happened since the pits closed down is a lot of miners have now taken up employment with Lothian Health Board. There's a different sense of being between ex-miners and other people.

I know that if I go to a branch meeting asking for a strike and was able to convince the ex-miners that work there it was the right thing to do. I know they would back me and they would argue the case. But with people from out with the mining industry it's harder to argue the case because they don't have the same kind of background, they didnae live it.

I miss the pit, I miss the work. I don't miss the shifts but I certainly miss the people I worked with, even the ones that scabbed. Some of them.

The last ten years should show people what the government is capable off. It's not about democracy – it's about big companies decimating industries like the mining industry, decimating industries like the steel industry. And they're quite happy for this country to become the Taiwan of Europe. Quite happy to see skilled workers like miners on the broo.

One thing that the year-long strike did is that it delayed the closures. It gave people another year or two's employment. It was a heavy price to pay for it, but it was worth paying. I don't regret anything that I ever did during that strike. If the same situation arose today, in the hospitals and I felt that the only way to resolve it was to go out on strike then that's what I would do. Strike action was correct then and it's correct now and it always will be correct. It's our last weapon. But it's something you don't take lightly.

JOE OWENS

Blackburn

I started in Riddochill Colliery in 1942 and I served an electrical apprentiship there. I worked there for twenty-seven years until they closed it, obviously because the M8 motorway was passing the pit gate.

I was transferred to Whitrigg Colliery which had less coal than Riddochill had when they closed it. After three and a half years they closed Whitrigg and, thinking I was doing myself a favour, I went to the British Leyland in Bathgate and discovered that I couldn't afford to work in it, having six of a family and being continually laid-off for one reason or another. Eventually, after suffering it for six years, I phoned Polkemmet Colliery and was asked up there for an interview and got started as an electrician there. That was in 1978.

I was in Polkemmet when the miner's strike started, which proved to be a strain on the whole family after a few months. I received no money of any description. There were eight of us in the house and the only money was from a part-time job my wife had. But due to the generosity of neighbours and friends there was always plenty of food. People would open the front door and leave a parcel and we wouldn't even know who it was. The first Christmas of the strike, that's when the strike had been going seven or eight months, the house was full of food, chickens and everything handed in by people.

Eventually, when the strike finished, I went back to Polkemmet. We were then transferred to Bilston Colliery in 1985 and I worked there for roughly about three years when the opportunity to take redundancy came. Being at the age I was, I was getting more benefit taking it then rather than waiting to retiring age. It turned out that I was only a year out on redundancy when they closed Bilston.

I was then at an age when you couldn't get a job – over sixty – so since that I've been unemployed and I'm now past retiring age anyway. As far as the closure of different collieries that I've been in is concerned, Riddochill, without a doubt, was closed because the motorway was going by the pit gate. They transferred us to a pit in Whitrigg where there was hardly any coal. We were scraping for coal to keep it going until they were forced to close it. And they closed Polkemmet Colliery and transferred us to a worse pit with less coal, Bilston Glen.

Polkemmet Colliery was flooded due to a deliberate criminal act. Millions of pounds worth of plant destroyed just because a man dropped a switch on the surface. For his criminal act he was promoted by the Coal Board because it suited their ends. That was the whole outlook of the Coal Board at that time, there was promotion going if you could close a colliery. That was my opinion of the whole thing anyway.

The strike, I suppose, was necessary, but the only thing I think was wrong was that it was prolonged past the time when there could have been a workable settlement. After about six months I think they could have settled up and the union would still have had some power left. Due to it going the distance it went, a year and a day as far as Polkemmet is concerned, it actually destroyed the union and I think that's the only fault I've got with Arthur Scargill: that he could have saved face and kept the union with some power if he had settled earlier. In my opinion, if Mick McGahey had been in Scargill's job, it would have been settled in June or July and he's more or less said that in his own words since.

The strain of the strike was terrific, with no money coming in the house and eight people to be fed and, as I say, only the generosity of neighbours and friends solved that problem.

There's no doubt about the strike being actually organised by the Tory Party, because the Ridley Report which was written years before the strike laid out the plans and they were carried out to the letter. There's never been as many policemen in Britain as there was during the miners' strike. They've disappeared since. There's a shortage of policemen and yet there were thousands available when the miners' strike was on trying to browbeat the miners. There have been cases proved where it was men taken out of the army and obviously that was what happened because these policemen are not available now.

It was just a browbeating affair – beat them into the ground and be prepared to bankrupt the country to beat the miners, knowing that if they beat the miners every union in Britain was beat. If the other unions had had any foresight or their leaders any intelligence, they would have been backing the miners up and they would have some power now which they have got. They've got no power just due to the fact that they didn't support the miners.

Polkemmet Colliery was supplying coal directly; it wasn't taking time to hit the ground, to Ravenscraig. And when the miners asked the men at Ravenscraig not to accept imported coal, they just put the fingers up at them, which was another contributing factor to the closure of Polkemmet. Since that event, of course, Ravenscraig has been closed and they're looking for everybody's sympathy after turning down the miners' appeals.

I've no sympathy for them, same as I've none for the Nottinghamshire miners. I'm actually praying for pits to close in Nottingham so that I can laugh at them. I'm bitter about lack of support from other unions. I'm bitter about the Government-initiated union, the UDM, actually started with money from the Government simply to break the NUM. It's never been heard of in history: a government-instituted union. For a government that hated unions then supplying money to start one up is a turn-up for the books.

The men who are the leading lights in the UDM, coming from Nottingham, were just doing what their fathers did in the 1926 strike when they beat the miners then tae. It was just a sort of tradition with them. They were born to be blacklegs actually, it's bred into them. So now when I see them appealing for help because they're closing pits in Nottingham, it gives me great satisfaction.

The greatest effect the strike had on me was trying to fathom out the thinking of the men who went back to work during the strike, boys that you knew. They still look at you wondering if you're going to speak to them or not, which I do. But they know that I know they're blacklegs and they've got that to live with for the rest of their lives. I mean, there's nothing can alter that.

Other than that, the strain that was on Jane during the strike was terrific. She was under extreme pressure trying to keep the household together as far as feeding everybody was concerned, paying rent and other bills that had to be paid and it was just extremely difficult and she was under terrific strain. Her nerves were shattered, actually, with the pressure of everyday life. But, since that, we've made a recovery alright and it's now behind us, but I wouldn't wish that on anybody.

We were living under extreme capitalism, actually, and that's an evil in itself. There's no end to what can happen to working people under this Government, so we've just got to wait and see what's going to happen next.

The availability of work was nil for a while for young people here. It's only lately, with the emergence of some of these Japanese and American factories that jobs have been created. There was certainly nothing for young men for a while in this area. Young boys were guaranteed work here when they left the school because there were so many pits. There are young men who have left the school now and they are in their twenties and never had a job, they don't know what it is to get up and go to work.

There's a lot of things stick in my mind about the strike, I'm talking about suicides and killings – through frustration. I can always mind of the time when you* had come in and told me that you had been arrested on the picket line and you had to go to Dunfermline. These things are all added pressure to your mother and I wondering what was going to happen there. There's so many bad things happened during the strike it's hard to forget them.

I remember the social worker arriving, sent by the court to look into your background, family life and what sort of life you led to decide what sentence to pass on you. The social worker was actually 100 per cent behind you. The idea of this happening, social workers coming to see what sort of family life you had, what sort of house you lived in was totally upsetting, especially to your mother.

I don't regret the strike; I regret the time it lasted. I think it went by its use-by date. It got to the stage where it broke the union rather than breaking the government.

*the editor

JACKIE AITCHISON

Dalkeith

I suppose I could describe myself as a product of being born at the bottom of the bing.

I was born in a mining area through in the West of Scotland in 1947. The coal industry there came to a sudden end 'round about the early 50's and my father became an industrial gypsy, moving through to the Lothian coalfield to further his mining career and I came though as a school laddie.

When I left school, with no qualifications, I took up an apprenticeship in engineering but I was paid off after about six months with about 200 other people. If people cast their mind back there was a wee bit of a recession in the early 1960s.

I took up various jobs, working in engineering and the building trade. I was involved in nursing for a wee while, was in the fire brigade, drove ambulances, various jobs. I went into the pits in 1969. I went to Bilston Colliery, one of the big super pits at that particular time, a million tonner with a life expectancy then of about a hundred to a hundred and fifty years.

I became just an ordinary miner, married with a young family, with no ambitions other than looking for a bit of overtime at the weekends. There were times when seven days a week wasn't enough to try and earn some extra cash to support my family.

I suppose I was always on the fringes of being a union activist. I got involved in various local disputes in as much as giving my support if it meant everybody going home and losing a day's wages to prove a point with management.

I became further involved in the union, just as a matter of interest, from my family background – my father was a great union activist. I became more and more interested in the union and became the colliery representative for the Area Safety Committee and, after serving there for a couple of years I was appointed for one year as a Scottish representative on the Safety Committee.

That really aroused my interest in the trade union movement. I was sent to union schools, I began to learn a bit more, I began to read a bit more about the history of my industry and, I suppose a spin off from that, the history of the working class in general.

In the early 1980s, I became somewhat disillusioned with the representation from people within the union in Bilston Glen and began to challenge for certain positions. I had no ambitions to be a union official – all I wanted to be was a part of the union committee, part of the collective. However, in 1982, one of the officials of the union, the secretary of the branch, announced, quite openly, at a monthly union meeting, that if the chance of redundancy came along he would grasp it with both hands and he would fight anybody who would try and interfere with that.

This was totally against everything that I believed in and I challenged him for his position on that basis. And, quite surprisingly, I was elected secretary of the branch. I suppose Bilston Glen at that particular time was the largest colliery in Scotland, the largest unit, and the secretaryship carried a great deal of power and, overnight, I became known throughout the Scottish NUM.

Along came the national strike of '84/'85 and it's my opinion that all the resources that the coal board could muster to try and break the strike in Scotland were pushed towards breaking the strike at Bilston Glen. We were obviously the largest colliery, the largest unit – if you can break that, then there was every chance that the whole of the Scottish strike would fold as well.

It was an extremely long, difficult strike, as every miner in Britain who went through the strike will testify. But certainly the pressures at Bilston Glen were at times horrendous. Every new angle that British Coal could think of to break the strike was tried at Bilston Glen first: personal contact by senior management, going and chapping men's doors late at night asking them to come back; inducing them with various monetary promises to get them to go back; attempting to discredit the union officials at every possible turn; arrests that took place on trumped-up charges that were later dismissed from court.

The majority of cases didn't even go to court; they suddenly couldn't find the arresting officers. All sorts of ploys were adopted by the Establishment and by British Coal.

It's been said to me from time to time that because of my approach and my behaviour at Bilston, we kept a lot of men out. They couldn't point a finger at me and say I had benefitted in any way through the union, it's just that I believed quite honestly in the principles of what the union was trying to achieve.

I suspect that British Coal realised this was happening because in September of 1984, six months into the strike, I was dismissed for allegedly being involved in gross industrial misconduct.

Basically all I did was step over a white line that was painted on the roadway outside the colliery, which British Coal had identified as part of the colliery and therefore I had no right to be standing there. It was later proved that this infamous white line had absolutely nothing to do with British Coal property, it was the property of the local regional authority.

However, it made no difference, I was summarily dismissed. After the return to work in March 1985, I tried through various avenues to get my job back. Ultimately, I went to an industrial tribunal and after three days of arguments, it was unanimously found in my favour that I should be reinstated in my job.

At no time did I pursue any compensation. All along I wanted reinstated back in my job. Unfortunately, under industrial legislation in Great Britain, even if it's found in an employee's favour, there is no legal obligation on the part of the employer to take you back.

Twelve months later, British Coal applied to the industrial tribunal for a compensation settlement. In other words, they had no intentions of taking me back. Although I was innocent they just wanted to pay me off with compensation.

At that particular time, after some eighteen years of my life being invested in the coal industry, I was awarded the large sum of £7,200 minus any DHSS payments, any unemployment benefit payments, income tax and pension. It was all taken off it, so I ended up with just over £4,000.

Since then, I've worked out just exactly what I lost. Had I been reinstated back in my job in 1985, until 1988 when the colliery closed, I should have been earning, on average, £10,000 a year, so that's £30,000 I've lost. Plus a redundancy payment of £24,000 – so in total, I suppose I lost £54,000. It made me extremely bitter towards the management that existed within my industry.

Well, since 1985 I pursued various other avenues to gain some employment. I tried everything. Anything that I thought I could do whether I was qualified or not, I applied for. Sometimes I got to the interview stage, but most times I received an acknowledgement of my application and it went no further.

I suspect that a blacklist existed and I was part of that blacklist. I couldn't gain employment any place. I even believe it affected my family, because two of my sons and my daughter, who certainly had, as far as I'm concerned, good educational qualifications, were totally ignored by various prospective employers.

Not being able to get a job isn't very nice. I've never been out of work in my life. It was certainly having an effect on my confidence and making me more irritable and making me more embittered. Not bitter towards my industry; I always loved and still do love the coal mining industry. I still believe there's a very bright future for the coal industry. But certainly it cemented a suspicion that I've held for a long number of years that the management of the industry is totally deplorable. And let me qualify that. I also recognise that everybody has played a part in what's happened to the coal mining industry. It's so easy to blame management. But being a nationalised industry, not enough of us took enough interest and politicians took the easy option of sticking their head in the sand and ignoring what was happening to the industry. It was badly, badly run. And I think we all have to shoulder a wee bit of the blame for it because we ignored certain things that were standing out like a sore thumb.

However, as I said, I still love the industry. With that in mind I decided to become involved again. I never lost my feelings for it, you know. I always knew that somehow I would get back into mining. I didn't think what's happened now would possibly be the solution at that particular time, but I just knew somehow I would get back into mining. I had left too much feelings in the industry and that's awfy personal to me.

British Coal, I suppose, robbed me of my livelihood. One thing they canny rob me off, and no one can rob me off, is my integrity and my honesty and my feelings: they're very, very personal to me.

I couldn't find a job any place. And I suppose one of the only qualifications I had in my life was a driving licence and I've always thought myself rather a good driver. If that sounds vain, so be it.

Anyway, my wife started saving some money and right out of the blue she announced she'd raised enough to put me on a course for driving buses, to go for my PSV licence. So she'd paid for me going for it and I suppose that was the wee incentive for me to pass. I thought it was hell of a good, touching, very marvellous what she had done. (Bear in mind, she still had a family to raise and she saved that off part-time wages as a home help.)

However, I was successful. I passed my driving test to become a double-decker driver. But things didn't improve straight away because I found then I was still blacklisted. I couldn't get a job with major driving establishments and national bus firms or the local passenger service buses. However, there was a small firm quite close to the colliery that used to do a great deal of union work and I suppose the influence of a wee bit of loyalty paid off because they took me on as a part-time driver.

During certain parts of the busy season and the summer I was taken on on a full-time basis. But even after my wife made certain sacrifices and paid for me to get this licence I quickly discovered that my heart certainly wasn't in driving buses for a living for the rest of my life.

As time went on from 1985, the Scottish industry was running down on near enough a daily basis. There were collieries closing or there were small units closing or collieries were paying off a hundred men here and a hundred men there. And it was still disgusting me and I still had this driving ambition to get back into the industry.

The colliery that I spent most of my working life in came under serious threat in 1988 and I attended all the rallies and all the meetings. It was the usual rhetoric that I had heard for years, absolutely nothing new. Bilston Glen went down without much of a fight and I believe it was sacrificed to save what was left of the Fife coalfield. I don't know how history will record it but I believe a more strenuous campaign could have been conducted to save it.

Since then there's been absolutely no new industry moved in to take up the slack of these men who were made redundant and I suppose more importantly, nothing has been offered or planned for future generations coming along. Where do people get employment?

Around about that time I bumped into an old colleague of mine who had been kicking round the idea of workers' cooperatives, even when I knew him in the 1970s, being an alternative to the bad management practices that existed within our industry.

Monktonhall Colliery was the sister colliery of Bilston Glen, another large density employer with 2,500 men in its heyday and a million ton output. That colliery hadn't been closed; it was placed on a care and maintenance basis with an agreement with the union and British Coal that it would be reviewed sometime in 1991.

So from 1988 to 1991 we had to work very, very hard to upgrade a feasibility study of what we could do at Monktonhall.

On 9th June 1992 we officially took over the running of Monktonhall as a miners' cooperative and we have been involved up until now. We've went through a very, very hard exercise in recruitment and developing the colliery. When we announced that we had intentions of convincing British Coal to give us the colliery, we announced to anyone that wanted to join our cooperative that the price of joining was £2000, and that meant everybody.

However, the government and our financial backers told us that the £2,000 didn't qualify as a substantial commitment from the men and to really convince these people to come up with the financial backing, we would need a substantial increase to demonstrate that the commitment for the men was certainly there.

So, after a lot of heartsearching, a lot of tough arguing, a lot of tough discussing we arrived at the figure of £10,000 which we correctly presumed would convince big financial backers that the commitment was certainly there from the men. There are very, very few men with that kind of money lying around, the majority of them had to go and borrow it from banks, building societies and financial institutions.

I don't accept for one minute that men bought their jobs. The guys who are involved in our project are actually equal owners in a business. I suspect it's possibly, under the present political regime, the only alternative to save what's left of the Scottish mining industry. Certainly, it's the only alternative to save what's left of the Lothian's coalfield.

Midlothian ten years ago? Well, I would say it was a very prosperous little county. Plenty jobs, especially in the mining industry, I suppose there was six to six and a half thousand jobs, guaranteed jobs. At that time, everybody thought, very, very long term jobs.

You could plan your future. Nobody thought anything about buying their house, buying a new car, going on holidays abroad. Planning for the future.

I suppose the most important thing was, miners knew perfectly well there was going to be jobs for their sons. There was enough in natural wastage from the colliery to take up the young lads who were leaving school. It was a bright future in the industry.

All those jobs are now lost, all those aspirations are now lost, all the plans for the future are now lost. Where do we take up the slack? What do we offer kids now? I also think there's another thing too, a very important factor: people's confidence. Because of what's happened to the traditional high employer in the area, now that it's virtually gone and all that's left is the project we're involved in it's destroyed a lot of people's confidence in just exactly what can happen.

There was a lot of good things within the industry I would like to see coming back. When you think of what we did for the old people, looked after them, took them on trips twice a year, made sure they were okay. It's what we did for the young too, that's the most important thing. We looked after majorettes, we looked after boys' clubs, we looked after girls' clubs, we sent kids away on adventure training, we sent kids abroad.

We produced some of the greatest athletes in the world through the mining industry, some of the greatest sportsmen. And not only did we back them morally and principally, but more importantly we backed them financially. And that's what the mining industry did, it was us that did it, and I would just like to see a wee bit of that coming back.

I don't know what the answer is. One small answer to it is what I'm involved in Monktonhall just now. I only wish there was 10,000 jobs there, but there's no'. The reality is there's only two or three hundred jobs there. But it's two or three hundred more than nothing.

ALEX SHANKS

Edinburgh

I worked in the pits for nine years. I started in 1980 and was made redundant in 1989. I worked in Monktonhall until January '89 and then had a brief spell at Bilston Glen.

My main impression about the strike is that it was right. I don't know if there's a lot of people who would say that. I think one of the other main things nobody can forget is that, despite the fact it was right, it ended in a defeat. But, in my opinion, that doesn't totally rule out the idea that struggling to defend your job is fundamentally right despite the fact that the outcome wasn't satisfactory to the huge majority of miners and their families.

My main memory of the strike is of people coming thegether to organise in the communities, the solidarity with each other, the soup kitchens that were set up to provide people with a living, the collections made on the street and the support from huge sections of society.

I could give you a few examples of collecting on the street: where a single parent in Edinburgh gave me a fiver once out of her giro; of Dryborough's Brewery in Craigmillar donating the beer they got on top of their wages to Newcraighall Strike Committee and other examples like that of ordinary people supporting the miners' cause.

I think the other memory is that while a lot of people seek to blame Arthur Scargill, most recently I remember Bill Jordan saying that he was the captain of the Titanic, it wasn't just the responsibility of Scargill to lead the miners to victory, it was also the responsibility of people like Bill Jordan, whose members, in my opinion anyway, supported the miners. His members saw the link between the coal industry, the backbone of British industry, and engineering. These people bear the brunt of the responsibility for the miners going down to defeat.

People like Scargill and the miners' families tried their damndest but these people didn't actually provide support. I think, as well, that the ferociousness of the response from the Tories, the government, the state and everything against the miners, pointed out to me, which is a memory that will never be forgotten through the whole of my life, the class nature of society.

All the miners and their families were demanding, basically, was the right to work 3,000 feet under the ground to provide themselves with a wage in order to live. Not in an exuberant way, but in a normal way, maybe to have a TV, to have a video, a car and maybe one foreign holiday a year. For the Tories that was extreme and they used the police, the courts, the media and whatever else they had at their disposal to make sure that the miners weren't entitled to them, in fact to make sure the miners spent a lifetime on the dole.

Sometimes, when you look back on your life it's hard to name one individual incident, but obviously it changes your life. When you're on strike for a whole year without any income and if you're prepared to see that through to the end, then that has a long-lasting effect on you.

Monktonhall was on strike eight weeks before the national strike in October/November 1983, and because of that I started to think in a certain way about how society should be run. I'm of the opinion that, unconsciously in most people and consciously in some, your outlook in relation to the way society is run, and the way politics is, shapes the way in which you look at your personal life. So, I think that the miners' strike and everything that happened in it certainly did change my outlook on how things should be run in society.

Prior to the strike I was quite young, I was only nineteen and still an apprentice. Prior to the Monktonhall strike I had absolutely no involvement politically or in the trade union. I didn't even attend trade union meetings. But when the Monktonhall strike came about, after it I became youth delegate for SCEBTA at the pit and I began to take an active interest in trade unionism and politics. Shortly after that I decided to become a supporter of the Militant. I joined the Labour Party first and then decided to affiliate myself with the *Militant* newspaper in the party at that time.

I think the experience of the strike consolidated everything that I felt in relation tae the need for a strong trade union, the need for a strong involvement by the rank and file, the ordinary members, so that the movement could go in the direction that they wanted.

The large majority of miners went back to work proud, those that had stayed out for a year. I think there's a section that would have stayed out even longer and there are some who would have stayed out as long as it took, although it was getting increasingly difficult. There was a recognition very quickly that the strike had been a defeat and that we hadn't made any concrete gains and we hadn't got an agreement as far as pit closures was concerned.

It also became fairly obvious that because the miners had been on strike for a year that the workforce was basically tired, they weren't prepared to take any more industrial action immediately and therefore it was clear that the management had the upper hand.

The immediate aftermath of the return to work was marked by a divided workforce at pits like Monktonhall at which I would say the majority of the men managed to stay out, although it was quite close by the end. As time went on that began to heal to the extent that people were prepared to try and get on as far as the work was concerned. But there wouldn't be many miners who would enjoy going for a pint with a scab.

That was my attitude with the trade union. I might not agree with somebody that had went back to their work and I wished they had stayed out, but as far as me representing them in any capacity was concerned you had to try and rebuild the unity of the union.

The unfortunate thing about the pit closures was that it became a news item that wasn't really worth reporting on the national news because there were that many. Pit closures became an everyday event and therefore the devastation that occurred in the communities was sometimes lost, apart from on the people who were immediately involved.

Some miners did alright and survived, others didn't. Others found themselves in the position where they had bought a house, and paid off their mortgage, in a mining village but found that the village became a ghost town. They'd paid off their mortgage but couldn't get a job and couldn't sell the house, because why would somebody move into a mining village that hasn't got any prospects for work? They're trapped.

Personally, the long term was what I was always worried about: what would happen to the communities and ourselves once some of the redundancy money was gone. I only got about £5,000, which was nothing, well, short of half a year's wages. It wasn't a lot of money.

I was offered a transfer before I decided to take redundancy. The idea of moving south of the border into other parts of the coalfield wasn't particularly appealing. I viewed it as compulsory redundancy. I found myself working, more or less full-time after 1989 trying to build support for the Militant, which I did for three years, then, while still supporting the Militant I thought I should go and get a proper job.

I went to college and managed to get on a course which prepared me for a job in the oil industry and I've just started working offshore. I've only been off once at the moment but it's heavy industry, which I find myself at home in. But at the same time being two weeks away from home is particularly difficult. I don't find the oil industry in many ways much different from working underground.

I don't think that you could speak to any miner who wouldn't miss something about the pit. The huge majority probably don't miss working 3,000 feet under the ground trying to get coal out, but at the same time, because of the history of the miners in Britain I think there was a special sense of community and solidarity. We always got a good laugh and a good crack when you were in the pit with your mates.

I think if I had the opportunity to go back to a pit I would, although I wouldn't be particularly keen to go back to a private pit or a consortium like the guys at Monktonhall.

Although people reading this may say: 'Aw, this is just a political activist speakin,' I was actually shocked and disgusted at the way in which a government would try and get their way in relation to the miners who, with their families, hadn't done anything wrong.

I'm bitter about that. I'm bitter, as a person who had no previous offences, about being dragged through a court for being on a picket line and getting fined £200 for a first offence breach of the peace.

I'm bitter about people you would expect to be on your side like those in the leadership of the Labour Party and the trade unions who in my opinion have it in their power to deliver active support to people in struggle making excuses that they can't deliver. I feel that every time people point the finger at Scargill they point the finger at the miners because in my opinion the miners were reluctant followers of Scargill and only fought when they were absolutely convinced that what he was saying about 70 pits and 70,000 jobs was right.

People go on about the ballot, and I think there should have been one for tactical reasons, but you can't convince me that Arthur Scargill and the NEC kept 100,000 miners on strike against their will.

I'm bitter against fellow miners who consciously tried tae break the union and set up another union, the UDM. Most of the other miners I think were wrong to go back and I wouldn't like to spend a long time socialising with them but apart from that all is forgiven, basically.

For ten years now the leaders of the movement have been point-ing to the strike and saying – look what happened to the miners and if they can't win, who can win? It's about time they said that the great thing about the miners' strike was that they were prepared to have a go. The people who were involved will never forget what happened, it's left its mark.

STIRLINGSHIRE

JOHN McCORMACK

Fallin

I'm aged sixty. I'm a married man wi' one of a family and one granddaughter, and they a' stay in Fallin. My son-in-law works wi' the Stirling County Council; otherwise, if the pit had still been going I suppose he would have been a miner the same as the rest of them.

I started the pit in 1947. I'd been in the pit about thirty-eight years, that was up until 1985 when I was made redundant. I left the school at fifteen and went straight to the pit. I left the school on the Friday and I started the pit on the Monday, it was at the Christmas time. And when you went to get a job at the pit at that time there was nae such things as medicals etc; a' you did was you saw the surface foreman and he asked your name, asked who yer faither was an' if he kent your faither then you got a job in the pit and that's how I started in the pit.

Fallin's always been a village pit. When I say a village pit we also had, just along the road, well, we had Polmaise One and Two, and this pit here in the village was Polmaise Three and Four. And the two o' them were linked up underground wi' a tunnel. You could go fae wan pit tae the other. They used to be walked, I think it was once or twice a week, to make sure the road was alright.

I worked on the surface for years, I would say maybe about four or five years, then underground about nineteen tae the oncost and I was on the oncost till I did my training. And along wi' being underground at the pit I also played professional football which meant that I had to get a job constant backshift. I played wi' Falkirk FC. I played wi' Falkirk fae 1953 to 1960 and they won the Scottish Cup in 1957. Although I wasnae part o' the Cup winning team I was there as part o' the squad.

I have always, and I don't know if it's very important or no', but even to this day I always wear a collar and tie. Miners are always recognised by mufflers and scarfs. I'm going back tae the days when I started in the pit, gaun hame wi' your pit boots on and your black een, things like that. I can always remember the first day I started in the pit, myself and a boy by the name o' Shug Brown, he started as an electrician; I just started as an ordinary miner. And we went across tae the Miners' Welfare wi' our pit boots on, it was the custom at that time tae come hame wi' your pit boots on; naebody left their pit boots at the pit.

We had always been wanting to have a game at snooker in the Miners' Welfare and we couldnae get a game because of our age. We were allowed in but we were never allowed to play. The hallkeeper was an old ex-miner, Bob Hutton, and we put our names down.

It was on a Monday at five o'clock when the Welfare opened.

There were two tables. He looked up the book. He says, 'You'll be playing on Friday at nine o'clock.' So we had to wait till Friday at nine o'clock. When the two of us went for our cue he says 'Let us see your hands.' He told us to go and wash our hands. By the time we came back after washing our hands another two miners were on the table. We had to call him Mr Hutton, you couldnae call him Bob. 'Mr Hutton, there's somebody on the table.' 'Aye' he says, 'you're too late, put your name back down again.' So we put our names back down again and we didnae get a game till the following Wednesday. So that was my first experience o' the pit.

When I started the pit at first, on the pithead, I really liked it. That was all we really knew. If you were a miner you went to the pit, you didnae bother about anything else. Then I went down the pit, as I said, after about four years on the surface. We went to Bo'ness, as far as Bo'ness, to dae our underground training. We used to go there once a week, that was pretty good. Then I got a job in a section, 17 Section. The talk at the pit was that it was bad enough fighting the Germans without stealing their coal, the section was that far away. I can always recall going away down there, it was maybe three, four miles fae the pit bottom, and you couldnae bear the heat. In fact as you were walking tae your work you were taking garments aff.

The jacket was aff at the top o' the brae. By the time you got tae your work all you had on was your boots and your trousers and your kneepads. Some colliers worked wi' just their pants on, it was that warm. They even sent a barrel o' water down there and you could go and fill your flask. By the time it got down to the section it was warm.

There was a time when I was down there I even thought about joining the army. I don't know whether it was the distance we were walking or what it was, but I took a scunner to the pit and for quite a number o' months I was looking round about for pals to see if somebody would join the army wi' me. Inwardly my heart wasnae really in leaving the pit but I believe if somebody had said, 'come on we'll join up', I would've went. Anyway, it didnae materialise and after a period of time I got a chance to dae my face training, brushing the coal, pan-shifting and all that.

As I said, I was playing the football so I had to stay on the constant backshift; I did my training in the morning in Falkirk. And when I went up there it was always wi' a collar and tie and fae that time tae the now, even sitting in the house, nae matter what day it is, the first thing I dae is get washed, shaved and put a collar and tie on.

On the whole I wouldnae change my life. I really enjoyed the pit; I enjoyed the company of the men I met o'er the years. At the same time as I started in the pit, I think Fallin was the first pit in Scotland, as far as I know, tae let the Poles in, that was in 1947. There were only two shafts at that time, Number Three and Number Four, and they were sunk in 1902. They sunk a further shaft, Number Five shaft sometime in the 50s. Fallin's the only pit I ever worked in. I remember going into the pit, a typical cheeky laddie and telling the bath attendant I want a downstairs locker and him telling me I'd get an upstairs locker and I had that from the day I went into the pit till the day I left, 459, I still remember the number.

For all the time I worked in the pit I couldnae really say, bar for that one twinge when I thought I wanted to join the army, that I didnae like the pit. And for all those years I couldnae say that anybody ever picked on me – I canny remember seeing anybody picking on anybody else. The comradeship in the pit was even better then than it was come '85 when I left. Maybe it was because at that time if there was nae jam in the canteen they were hame on strike and couldnae get a ba' out quick enough, fourteen or fifteen a side, playing for hours and hours.

I got involved in the union in 1971. I had always been union-wise, even at the school I always liked to see fair play. I was never the chairman, I was always the vice chairman. Our delegate at that time was a man called Terry McNeil; he was a good age, retiring age. So, he decided to take his retirement. When he was away as delegate to conferences I always stood in so when he packed in the miners automatically thought that I should then become delegate. I didnae want the delegate's job personally, I wanted to be in the union but I didnae want it. I actually thought that I wasnae capable o' daein the delegate's job. But now I can say that the delegate's job was quite an interesting one – I quite liked it and I could dae it without any bother, plus the fact I could get up and say a few words which was very important. If you couldnae dae those kind o' things you lose a bit of respect, I would say. I was the delegate for fourteen years at Fallin pit and in those fourteen years naebody ever stood against me. If anybody would've stood against me I wouldn't challenged them, I would have let them go.

However, everything went well. Quite a number o' times o'er those fourteen years I was approached by different individuals to join the Communist Party. I remember being down at Grunwick and a boy, I think his name was Gordon McLennan, I wouldnae be quite sure, approached me to join the Communist Party but I said no.

The only thing I had against the Communist Party was that when the top of the tree said aye everybody said aye. I'd be right in saying that some of them couldnae think for themselves. If they could think they were feart to show it or express it. That's how I saw it, but otherwise I had nothing against the Communist Party.

I don't think there was anybody in Polmaise pit in the Communist Party. I would also go as far to say that you could count on your hand, come the strike, how many men in the pit were members o' the Labour Party. I was never a member o' any party up until the strike then I joined the Labour Party but since that it's all fell away tae.

Before the Miners' Strike we hit a bad patch up here, we hit a fault. When we hit the fault Wheeler came to the pit and decided to take the main mine to the right and we knew the way that the fault was running that so far down this road we would hit it again;

this would be an excuse to shut the pit. He came to stop that mine, he decided to shut the pit down. He held a meeting with the NUM officials, that was McGahey, Bolton and Clarke on the Friday morning and Polmaise had to transfer men on the Monday morning to Castlehill and Solsgirth. So we held a meeting with Wheeler in the Miners' Welfare and I asked him to give us the opportunity to drive through the fault in the main mine.

The men, who were desperate for the place to go, were prepared to do the work without getting paid a bonus for it. So after a period of time he locked us out of the pit, at the end of June 1983; he locked us out for five weeks.

The reason was that the Cardowan men were coming to the pit and we wouldnae let them in. His excuse was that he was wanting to review the full pit. For that five weeks I took the token numbers of every man that worked in the pit and took the case to the manager. Within two seconds he said he wasnae paying so I sent that case to Geordie Bolton. He came to the pit and met the coal board agent along with myself and the manager. The Coal Board agent decided not to pay it. So the case went to the Umpire, it was a boy called Jack Kane, the ex-Lord Provost of Edinburgh and he upheld our case saying that we had turned up for work on a daily basis and the management had locked us out. We won our case and the figure they paid back was £45,000 – five weeks' wages each. So that didnae go down well with Wheeler.

Within four weeks we went through the fault; it was a fault we could master without any bother, back out onto the coal. We spent £22 million, the coal was six feet by six feet four all the way, there was only the one fault I've been talking about. They then came along and paid most of the men off. They only wanted a workforce of 117 men. At that time they were sort of running the show anyway, the Coal Board, it was as if the NUM had just flung the towel in.

So 300 men were paid off and the remaining boys drove the mines week out and week in, making good bonuses, and they just came along one fine day and shut it down for nae reason whatsoever. They required the money for the Barony. I would say that when they shut the pit down, section wise there was about ten to fifteen years' work.

Going back to when they were paying the men off, we decided to hold a meeting in the Miners' Welfare to see who was going, who wasnae going. The men agreed in the Miners' Welfare that you go out by age and by service, the oldest men were going out first. At that time I was about fifty. One of the boys had stood up and said that he would like the delegate to stay at the pit. I'd never been out of a job in my life, never signed on the broo or nothing in forty years and I was dubious about being out of a job. I didnae know what I was going to be daein' and I said that it had been agreed and at my age and with my service I was one of the first to go and I had to go. Anyway they decided that I should stay in the pit.

So I went and gave the manager the list of men who were staying in; it was after the Miners' Strike so me and him wasnae on, what would you say, speaking terms. He looked at it and said: 'Is that your name at the top up there?' I says: 'Aye.' And he got a red pen and wrote on it, I can always remember it: 'The big ship lollipop' with an arrow pointing to my name. He says: 'You're for the big ship lollipop, out.'

He rolled the list into a ball and threw it into the waste-paper basket and said he would decide who was going out the pit.

So the Coal Board then sent men through to tell us what we were due in redundancy payments. The manager said to me, 'You're going out the pit whether your name's on that list or no'.' He was keeping older men in and putting younger men out so I said right, if that's going to be it, naebody's going out. He started panicking. I said, 'If you want I'll call another meeting. You're the man who says there's to be 117 men in the pit and we've agreed to that and you're trying to make it awkward. So I'll be phoning Edinburgh.' He hummed and hawed and said, 'OK, but you're definitely going out.' By this time I was getting sick of him so I went back and told the men that I had to go out of the pit, that the manager was putting me out.

So they were taking the men in alphabetical order. So when it came my turn the boy said: 'Oh, the manager phoned o'er, John, you're no' to get out.' So I said that's OK then and went back over to see the manager. Aye, he says, you're getting out. So I went back o'er – same again. We were going back and forward two or three times. So I said to the chairman you go in that door, it had two doors, the manager's office, and I'll go in that door and we'll catch him. So we jammed the two doors so the manager didnae know where to run.

So I said it's make your mind up time, I'm either in the pit or out the pit, what's happening here? He says: 'You're out the pit.'

Before this I phoned Edinburgh and I got McGahey on the phone and I told him that the manager was making it awkward for quite a number o' men in the pit. I told Mick what was happening and he put me through to George Bolton who was agent for the area. He says, 'Look, you've won yourself a gold watch.' Patronising, ken. 'You've done well and, by the way, the Coal Board's running the show now and if the manager says you go, you go; if he says you stay, you stay.' I said that I was running about like a blue-arsed flea and he said, 'well, you'll have to sort that out yourself,' and that was the end of story. So that's what happened.

After that I still used to go up there every Thursday and Friday wi' a table outside collecting for the sacked miners and the miners who were working contributed. Although the money we got we didnae split it among the sacked miners; we sent to Edinburgh and they handed it back to the sacked miners.

Since the Miners Strike? At first I was lost, definitely lost. Just like when I was playing football – when I stopped I was demented, I didnae ken what to dae. I'm no' a gardener or anything like that.

As the months were going on I started to get involved, no' intentionally, but wi' people just coming along and saying, 'John, would you fill this form in for the DHSS?' and then when the thing came out for the industrial deafness for the miners I filled a' them in. If a miner dies I dae all the writing for the widow for her pension and coal and things like that. But o'er and above that I do nothing, I'm only in the house. I go to the Miners' Club on a Monday to sequence dancing. I go to the tap dancing on a Thursday o'er in Alloa and on a Saturday I go dancing in the Miners' Club. For hobbies, I go to the football, I like to go and see a good football match.

I've never worked since I left the pit. The closure of the pit has had a devastating effect on Fallin. I went to the pit straight fae the school. Most o' the laddies here were the same. You can go to the top o' the main road there any time and you'll get miners who could be working yet, young laddies who have never heard o' a job and there's nae work whatsoever here in Fallin. Nothing. The Coal Board's done absolutely nothing fae the pit shut down. There was a bit o' a haggle selling the property where the pit sat but I think the regional council are now in the process o' building units up there. I don't think it's small factories, I think it's for training people to work. But I think it's just a waste of money because it's only training people for a particular job and where are they going to get one after that?

Since the miners' strike I can honestly say I've been lost, absolutely lost. We talk about the pits, we talk about the Miners' Strike in particular. You hardly see any o' the miners now. I have been up at Timex to see what's going on up there and it's just something similar; in fact, I would say they're even getting it harder than we got it. I know what it's like being locked out and that was why I was up there. I was talking to people who were on strike. I didnae actually tell them I was a miner, I just told them I came from Stirling and was passing through.

I would have had another fifteen or sixteen years to work in the pit, it was a big loss personally but I would dae the same again. For the same cause I would dae the same again. On the whole I would say the miners did themselves proud during the strike. I would say tae that we had as many red indians* wi' the miners as we had wi' the police. I can sit and think o' things and burst out laughing. I've no regrets about the miners' strike. I'm no bitter. I'm no' even bitter wi' the Coal Board, I take that as part o' life and life doesn't run smoothly. I would say looking back, there's a different atmosphere, I feel different. I feel as if I've lost something. You cannae put your finger on it. I really miss the involvement o' the pit, that's what I really miss.

Some of the things that happened during the miners' strike you wouldnae believe. I sit there and think about the time we went to Ravenscraig and the police stopped all the buses, it was pouring wi' rain and they stopped the buses right at the gates, 'c'mon, get aff here, you're welcome here,' and we were wondering what was wrong. And after the demonstration was by we went to get the buses and they were ten miles away and we had to walk to get them. You're bitter at the time, you're angry at the time, but I'm no' angry now. You forget, ken, you forget quick.

* Battles

JIM ARMITAGE

Fallin

I started in the pit when I was fifteen and I'm fifty-nine noo. We worked doon the way. You don't work yourself up the way in the pit, you work yourself doon the way. I started working on the pit head on the tables then down the pit. After that working on the oncost and then gradually onto the face. Everybody's aim going doon the pit was to get a job on the face.

I was a coal-cutting machineman and I got a job wi' my Da' when I was eighteen and worked there for fourteen years wi' him. Then the power loading came into the pit where the coal was getting cut and loaded at the same time, you just worked the apparatus. That was a great step forward for the miners. You had a power loading team and our team stayed thegether for years and years, the same team, an' it was great, great laughs, great camaraderie.

The '84 one, that was a real stinker o' a strike. The fact was that we wernae a' oot and the government seized on this. They spent billions, no' millions, tae beat us which, everybody kens, they did. Got beat then back to work. A completely different situation a' thegether.

Actually that union up there was away ahead o' its time because, John was the delegate and I was the branch secretary, an' before he took o'er that job, an' this is without a word o' a lie, we were idle, on strike, every weekend. The least wee thing. Nae soap in the baths: we were hame – on strike.

They talk aboot the unions. After he got the job as delegate and me as branch secretary there was never another strike in that pit until it shut, bar the big yins. There wasnae a weekend lost on strike in that pit because we actually took a lot tae dae wi' the running o' the pit. John controlled the rest days. Boys used to go tae the management for rest days and they would turn them doon for nae reason. If they came to us they got them.

I worked for aboot a year after the big strike and was made redundant. Actually I've never done nothing since. I miss the pit. Before the strike it was great, a great pit, great place to work. But then when we got beat in the strike they put the boot intae ye. The unions were beat. You just couldnae turn round and say, 'You're no' daein that', because they could do it. They had the power, the mandate aff the government to dae what they wanted. And they did what they wanted.

There's still mair coal lying inbelow up there than was ever taken oot it. Anyway we were made redundant. We a' had our wee fling. I had my wee fling anyway wi' the dough. The things we were denied during the strike when we were skint, cleared up a lot o' debts, family debts and things like that. Bought a new car. I've just dodged away ever since.

They're daein that pit up there just now, they're landscaping it a' and making it into pleasure walks. You think that it took ninety years work up there to put that bing there, the slag heap, and these boys took it away in three months. An' you think o' a' the guys that worked below. Ken, you're walking o'er the top o' the place you used to work and you're saying to yourself 'I mind o' this section and I mind o' that section,' and you mind o' a certain man. Ken, there's a lot o' them dead and gone now. It brings back a lot o' memories, a lot o' sad memories tae.

I was fifty when we got horsed out. I had my son working in the pit up there, my son-in-law, ken they were a' a close knit company. And everybody was affected by it in a lot o' different ways. Fifty year-old and that's you on the scrapheap. They learnt you how to mine coal an' look after yourself in a pit but they never learnt you how to look after your money.

Boys were skint in the village a year after it. Their redundancy money was all gone. On the dole. Nae work o' nae kind. You drive through the village and there's two pubs, three if you count the club and that's about all there is. There's nothing.

The pit was the hub o' the village and it was a close-knit community. During that pit's lifetime it was really good. People could go oot the door an' just draw the door shut an' away tae the club. There was nae fear o' anybody banging your door in or anything like that. The atmosphere in the village changed. When the pit shut doon people drifted away, oot the village, and people drifted into different jobs, lost connection wi' each other as you would say. The camaraderie that was in the pit and used to be in the village, that disappeared.

Some o' us still meet thegether for a pint once a week and you get the patter and hark back to the laughs you used to get doon the pit. But the village has changed completely. From being a free and easy place now you're looking o'er your shoulders and locking your doors. If you've got anything somebody's going to wreck it tae, bar you watch it. It's because there's so many idle.

There's boys coming aff the school there and they stand at the corner for six weeks. If they stand there for six weeks they'll never work in their life. I've seen it happening. They're no' interested in working after that. And it's no' just six or seven, it's hundreds o' young laddies and lassies. There's nae work, nae work at a' and this is where the village life dies, in this village anyway. The pit held it thegether.

When I was young you worked in the pit, you gied your mother her dig money; you kept yours and maybe put something in the bank, which we a' did, ten bob a week in the bank. Young laddies that's going aboot nooadays havenae got a dink, never have had a dink, not a penny, nothing tae look forward tae. That's a shame.

People will blame the strike, even miners blame the strike, but the fact is that when our pit went back after the strike we started producing, breaking records. The coal that's in the pit up there would take about a hundred years tae mine. That wasnae the strike that caused that, it was a' lying lovely, ready for producing an' they come along and shut it. The coal's still there, who do you blame for that? You cannae blame the miners for they didnae have a say in that happening.

This has been a planned out affair, years back. In order to put this plan into fruition they had to break the miners first because everybody followed the miners. If they break them, well, that's it, which is true. My wife works in a canteen and I've seen boys working in they buses in there and they boys are absolutely terrified tae argue against the bosses. They do exactly what they're told whether it be fair or anything. Wi' me being used to working in the pit wi' a' the camaraderie I just couldnae work there, just couldnae work wi' that. But that's the national trend, no' just for they guys, that's for everybody.

When I was made redundant I could maybe have went across the water and worked, but I wouldnae go across there. I worked up in Fallin pit fae I was fifteen right up till I was fifty-one an' that was the pit shut an' I'd never been anywhere else.

The way it's affected me is that I've no' got as much money as I used tae hae. There's a lot o' things you miss oot on like going for a pint and buying something. That's another thing: you cannae just go in and buy a new fridge or a new telly or something like that, ken, the money's no' there. That's the bad side o' it as it affects me but the other side is I've got more time for fishing, I dae a good bit o' fishing.

That's the good side o' it, fishing and taking the grand-weans for a walk, unpaid! That's the material things you miss. Everytime your car's coming up for its MOT you're sweating. It's a' work you do yourself the now. Before you just put it into the garage, noo you learn how to sort it yourself. That's the killer bit about it.

When you get your redundancy money you expect to live quite nicely, you're expecting to be quite handsomely off. It doesnae work oot like that. No' for a stack o' boys, a lot o' boys. It runs oot quick. There's boys used to go to the pub at the weekend at least twice, you never see them noo. You maybe see them walking but never in the pub, which they liked. They liked the entertainment and a pint. They got their dough the same as us, but they spent it. Noo they're going tae rue it for the rest o' their days. It's been a sad experience for a lot o' boys.

I've got regrets about getting beat, a lot o' anger against people that let us doon, they Nottingham boys that worked. I thought a lot o' people were good tae us during the strike. Yarrows and that, they were really good tae us, we wouldnae have survived without them. You say to yourself, 'If, if . . . '. But all in all I've come out of it no' bad. It was a great experience. I was going to write a book one time about all my time in the pit. I wanted to write it a' doon. But I only wrote two pages and I couldnae get any further.

MARGARET ARMITAGE

Fallin

When the strike first started, we were quite a few weeks intae it before the women started anything. It was one night when we went to the club to a meeting and there was a woman there from somewhere else, I cannae rightly remember where she came fae, but she was talking about women who had been organised to help the men during the strike. So the women who were at that meeting decided that we would have a meeting of our own the following week, and that was where our committee was formed.

At the start I took on the secretary's job and what we termed ourselves was the Polmaise Wives Support Group. How we worked was we were our own unit working for Polmaise, but we had an area unit which was organised from Fishcross. There was a unit in Stirling, there was one for Polmaise here in Fallin, there was one from Bannockburn, one from Fishcross and there was one from Longannet way and the Fishcross unit was made up of two delegates from each of these groups. And then, they reported to the central women's group in Edinburgh. So it worked, basically, in the same way as the NUM.

Eventually, during the course o' the strike, I was on the Edinburgh committee as well. So I was actually secretary in this one and nearer the end o' the strike I was chairperson/secretary. I was also delegate tae the Fishcross one and I was delegate at Edinburgh. So my time was pretty much fully involved wi' the miners' strike at that particular time and the NUM and our unit worked sort o' hand in hand.

We got quite an awfy lot o' funds, simply for the sole reason that what we gathered in went immediately to the wives and families. There was an awful lot o' people who would just not donate anything at all if they thought it was going towards picketing. So our group really got a lot o' help because anything we got was distributed, not in money, but in goods, food vouchers or clothing or any necessaries.

There's quite a lot o' the villagers who weren't mining stock but who supported us because, in a mining community, everybody helps everybody; it's always been like that. I'm a miner's daughter, my sons were miners, my son-in-laws were miners and that's the type o' community it is. There was one time I was awfy disappointed. The STV cameras came, they had heard about our group an' the Polmaise pit and what have you, and they came to the club one night, it was always a Tuesday night when we ran a wee prize bingo. I had some baking and somebody else would make sandwiches and we charged so much. It a' made funds you see.

So the TV cameras came that night and there were one or two o' the women in the hall that night sitting having a drink and the cameras sort o' zoomed onto this, you know, which I thought was the wrong image because the women who were drinking were not miners' wives. So we sort o' fell oot wi' the STV folk that night, because I blew ma top. But it was one instance where you came up against things where the wrong image was getting put across.

And there were other cases where there were marriages wouldnae work because the women couldnae take the stress. I felt then our group tried to step in an' bring the women to our side an', not counselling, but I would say be supportive. You know, supportive conversation. And we did help oot quite a wee bit wi' families who were in difficulties and couldnae cope as well as others. Obviously everybody isnae made the same. In fact there was one death and that wee girl really needed help. Her man died during the strike, he was only a young chap and she was just left wi' a wee family. So these kindae cases got more help than others.

With the men themselves we started our Monday voucher scheme. That was where we had a list of every miner in the village, whether he worked in Polmaise or not, because there was quite a few o' them worked across the Fife side, and every week they came up to us and got a voucher for whichever amount o' money we could afford.

Sometimes they got three pound a week, sometimes they got four pound a week but voucher wise so they couldnae waste it on cigarettes or drink or whatever. And the local shopkeepers were very good wi' us, because they gave a concession. They never took the full amount so we were actually gaining a bit that way as well. And every shop got a cut. It would be the butcher's one week, maybe the greengrocer the next week or the grocery store the next week.

The local council helped out quite a bit because they gave a caravan which we billeted at the Argos entrance o' the Thistle Centre and that caravan was manned every day wi' women fae the village and donations were handed in there which was a big help as well. It's a pity noo there's some o' them split up because they couldnae stand the strain. And then the pit closing after it. We just thought – a' that fighting an' losing your job anyway, you know.

It's hard to describe noo the sense o' community feeling there was. In fact, we couldnae have sat in here an' sat ourselves down to a nice big meal if we knew the ones next door had nothing to eat. We would say – well, we've got this, come in wi' us. And the soup kitchens were another thing which the men's side organised.

They had the soup kitchen in the Welfare where miners and wives and families could go for a meal in the afternoon. We did our share o' picketing as well. We didnae go tae any o' the big mass pickets but if they were short o' pickets the women went onto the picket line with the men.

I would've said I changed from before the strike till during the strike, because I did things during the strike that I never thought I would have been capable of. I mean I went out and stood on platforms wi' speakers and made speeches and things I would never have thought I was capable of doing. But I did it and I travelled all over doing that type o' work to try and put the miners' families points o' view over. There was twice I appeared on television and that was something I would never have thought myself capable of doing.

But we coped. And then after the strike things took quite a wee while to get sort o' back to normal and we decided at the time that the women were going to stay together as a group, as a community group. But gradually it drifted off and drifted off and drifted off until it wasnae worthwhile keeping the group going any longer. I mean up until about two, three years after the strike I was still getting mail from Stirling groups, different groups, wanting to reorganise. But there wasnae the same interest.

There's an awfy lot o' women lost heart wi' the pit closing anyway. And then when the group finally broke up, well, I just sort o' drifted back into my normal routine and my normal way o' doing.

I felt I had a family and I had my grandchildren coming up. If I had a been a bit younger when this happened I may just have carried on. I even started taking an interest in the social work and I found that very interesting. But I felt it was just too late for me to start and take courses and things to qualify for that kind o' work. If I had been younger, yes.

I did it while it was necessary and I felt what I did, did help the miners' cause at the time. But afterwards I just felt that it wasnae worth carrying on. I would say that it did bring oot a lot in women who would never have thought themselves capable o' doing some o' the things that they did during the strike. And tae me that just showed their strength o' character. And they were prepared to battle on as long as the men were holding out, hoping we were going to win. And I still say Arthur Scargill was right. He's still right in what he's saying noo. I will say this though, if I had to do it again I would. If I had to do it again I would do the same things a' o'er again.

I still keep a' my books and things fae the strike, they're up the stair, and I'll no' part wi' them. We went to London, we went to Sheffield, we marched wi' the miners wherever they went.

I see a change now in so much that people like myself are falling back into their own wee niche and we're no' so much concerned about how the next family's doing. Mainly because now the pit's no here and our men are no' working thegether. Every other household noo has somebody idle in it. The pit's shut and all the factories round about are closed. All the wee industrial estates that had their wee working places are gradually closing down. That has made a change.

But because they're no' a' working together this family's no' concerned that Joe Soap's family doon the road their son's been made idle. They're no' in the same circumstances. During the strike everybody was in the same circumstances. We've no' got the same community spirit in the village now. I would say that the strike brought the whole village together. The pit was the hub and the village was the wheel, when the pit went the village went, that's how I still feel. When the hub went, the wheel just disintegrated.

It'll never be the same. I feel noo it'll be just a village wi' nae distinguishing thing about it. I think it's just going to be a suburb. It's no' the same as it used tae be, definitely no'.

ALEX McCALLUM

Fallin

I'm forty-two years of age. I started in the mining indus-try in 1967. My father and all my brothers were miners. I worked in the pit up until 1984 when I was sacked.

I was sacked for sitting down the pit, trying to save it fae getting shut. They did the same as at Polkemmet: they tried to flood it. There was talk at the time that they were going to try and shut Polmaise. Four boys had sat down the pit at Hemheath asking for a ballot for the strike, to get rid of Arthur Scargill. We decided then to do the same thing and also stop them fae flooding it. The consequences were that we got sacked and the four boys down in Hemheath got TV coverage and slap up meals, got away scot free.

When we came up the pit, I can always mind it, it was April, it was a Saturday morning and it was the day of the Grand National. I came up the Saturday and I got an envelope through on the Thursday morning with my P45 in it. We were the smallest pit o' the lot round about and we had the biggest amount o' men sacked.

We never had a scab at that pit. We didnae need to worry. Our job was actually round about trying to get scabs out o' other pits, because we didnae need tae worry about this village. It was a close knit community and naebody even thought about scabbing. That's the way the people up there think so they hit us hard.

Twelve of us from Polmaise were sacked; nine o' us actually went through industrial tribunals, which we won. At the end o' the day we got £12,000 each, across the board. Myself, and I would say about three or four other lads lost a lot o' money out of it, because if I had've came out the industry with my redundancy, I'd have qualified for £24,000. So, I actually got half of what I should have got. But at the end o' the day at least I came out wi' something, more than I can say for three other colleagues who got nothing.

We're talking about sacking men at sixty years old. They couldnae take the pressure – one died, one took a stroke. A man can work all his days in the mining industry, up till he's sixty years old, and that's what they done to them. That's the things that stick in my mind. We were young, I've got a chance, I can pick myself up and try and get a job. They boys had nae chance.

When we got settled up we asked them to gie him his coal [the miner who took the stroke] and they refused. He had won his case which proved that the man was right and the coal board were wrong for sacking him. When we pleaded a case for Bobby, none of the rest of us, not one of us, just coal for the auld boy and his wife, they refused. That's how bad it is.

It was four years before we actually got settled up, so it was a rough time, going through the strike and then coming into that. I had applied for jobs left, right and centre a' o'er the place and no' much success. The only chance we had was the Labour Party in Stirling who were really good to us. They made a statement up in the Miners' Club one time that they would stand by us and we'd never be out o' a job. So, we took them up on that and they stuck by their guns and gave us a job, but it was only temporary, no' full time. But there's three of us still wi' the council yet and one of them's myself, that's been since 1988.

But I've heard that there's a leaked letter saying there's £700 million to be cut from Scottish councils which will harm Scottish council workers' jobs and I've been told that Central Region has ninety days notice, if they don't win their tender they'll all lose their jobs. So, what's looked bright and rosy fae I started wi' the council is no longer.

After the strike I hung on hoping to get my job back. At the time we were fighting for our case we were going to court; three or four times we went with appeals. All the time we were actually hoping we would get our jobs back so I wasnae pushing it too much actually looking for a job.

I went for a job in Castlebridge wi' a private contractor. I gave them my full case but they said they weren't interested; if I could do the job that was it. They sent me to Cowdenbeath for a medical and I failed it through high blood pressure. I was on tablets for that up until I started work. Since I've started work I've been ta'en off them. But another boy had ta'en my place and he was sent for a medical and passed but they still didnae start him because, they said, it was still Coal Board premises. If it hadnae been Castlebridge and was a private mine there would maybe have been a chance, but because it was still run by British Coal they didnae start him. So, high blood pressure or no', I still dinnae think I would have got a start.

Looking at it now, I think we were sold right down the river. Sold right down the river. No' only by the scabs but even our ain executive. I'm talking about Geordie Bolton an' a' them. I can mind we were down in Sheffield and big Geordie Bolton standing on the balcony shouting 'What do we want?' and talking about going out on strike and daein this and that.

And still to this day he's stabbing Arthur Scargill in the back. Still to this day. And that was the kind of leader we were supposed to follow during the Miners' Strike. Gutless as far as I'm concerned.

I'd never been in London in my life, ye ken that, and I was actually there seven times during the strike. We went to Sheffield thirteen times. I ran about wi' John [McCormack] a lot, he calls me his minder. It was an experience and I met a lot o' people I would never have met. I enjoyed it, I'll tell you the now, and I'm no' kidding, I've lost a lot o' money, but I'd go back through it again. I would come back through it again. If we had had the backing then I know for a fact we would have won. She would have done a U-turn again. There's nae saying she wouldnae have come back again, but I say if the miners had stuck thegether . . . but you can go back to their records wi' the Spencer Union, their record's bloody deplorable and it'll always be the same.

Now when it begins to hurt them they're beginning to squeal like guinea pigs. I've still nae sympathy for them doon there, although they're miners and going to lose jobs and that, I've nae sympathy for them. I turn round and say – you deserve everything you get. I'm still bitter. I've got bitter feelings but at the end of the day if I went back again and I was still a miner I would dae it again.

There's actually disputes the now wi' the council and I'm prepared to dae it in there like I did it in the pit. Prepared to fight. I've been working class a' my life, all my days and I always will be because I've no' got the education tae get any further, no' at my age anyway, it's as simple as that. Got tae battle a' my days, got tae work a' my days.

There's nothing here, there's nae industry. Fallin has always been known as a militant area so who is going to bring industry into it? I cannae see any future for Fallin. You look about and they're standing at the top o' the road, there's nae jobs for them, it's unbelievable. Stirling's no' an industrial town, it's a tourist town, there's nae industry out here, so there's nae future for the folk out here.

There used to be a load o' pits round about here and the young yins were leaving school and going right in, at least it was a job. Nowadays there's nothing.

I still feel it. They knew that once she had destroyed us she would be out for the rest of them and it's happened. I was sitting here and I was disgusted really, even wi' myself, about how glad I was to see a place shutting down – Ravenscraig. Unbelievable. I was sitting sayin – 'gaun, ya beauty' – I was saying that and I shouldnae have been daein it, but what they did to us during that miners' strike was unbelievable. I'll never forget it.

I'll never forgive them. I could never forgive them. I had nae sympathy for them when they shut the place down. I shouldnae be like that against my fellow workers but that's the way it goes.

There'll need to be a general strike to get this Tory government out. There's a start, the miners merging wi' the railway workers and they're showing a wee bit of action now. Why no' the lot o' us. The truth. Why no' the lot of us and let's try and remove this lot because there's nae bloody future wi' this Tory government. Labour are making a mess of it tae. But I cannae see any better than Labour because the SNP have showed their true colours. But something will have to be done shortly because things have gone beyond a joke, beyond a joke.

My wife stood by me. She was on the committee, the women's committee. Two youngsters to bring up. It's hard, ken what I mean, it's like everything else, it's hard. She had a wee job wi' Stirling District Council. She eventually had to pack it in because they weren't prepared to gie us anything because o' the money she was making. But at the end of the day she got her job back wi' the council again, so she's there the now wi' the council, I'm wi' the council.

The two o' us working might end up wi' none of us working. To think, we were getting back on our feet, prepared to say we'll get this and we'll get that, prepared to go a wee holiday. Cannae even dae that now. You're feart. Nae security.

MARTHA McCALLUM

Fallin

My feelings were that they had a just cause to strike and it wasnae long fae the strike had started that they came home and told me that Alex was sitting underground to save the Coal Board fae sabotaging the pit.

So after, I think it was four or five days, he came home, he thought he still had his job, but he didn't have his job. At the time I was disappointed at the management side for going against someone that had roughly eighteen tae twenty years' service, a good attender. But, I mean, I wholeheartedly agreed wi' the strike, I supported it fully.

I went out and collected money. I went to Glasgow, I went to

London; I also went to distribute clothes and food, whatever we could do. It was a very hard time but I still would go through it a' again because I felt that their principles were right. It was a just cause and I wholeheartedly agreed wi' Arthur Scargill, I thought he was spot on as it proves its point now. But I would go through it a' again.

For me, I worked, so I had £32 a week. People had nothing. Alex got paid for Maureen and Stewart certainly, but I had taken other jobs tae keep our heads above water because I had things to pay, televisions, videos, because they were hired then. But it was a hard road, it definitely was. We felt it was never ending for us when after the first year went by he wasn't reinstated. The second year we knew there was no chance whatsoever. And he won his tribunal case after five years and that should have cleared his name, but it never, ever happened.

I'm bitter, really bitter. I still am bitter the way, no' just Alex, but a' the miners were treated, really very bitter. An' I cannae understand how these other miners wanted to work because, at the end of the day, it's come to them noo. If we had stood united, instead of breaking away into other unions, maybe we could have done it. An' also, I'm bitter wi' the biggest part o' the British public because they just didn't care because it wasn't happening to them. If they all had just united together and gave us even a week's stoppage, or something like that, we would'a' won it. Definitely.

It was a very close, very united village. I mean the biggest half o' the people participated in anything that was to help the miners. I was broken-hearted when they shut the pit, I mean I gret and gret because I never thought it would'a' happened but it had a terrible effect on the village, nae two ways aboot it.

I mean, you couldnae buy what you couldnae afford and that went on for a long time. All the miners were mair or less in the same boat but, its ta'en its toll, a few marriages, but at the end o' the day you've got to be strong, you're either wi' him or you're no' wi' him, ken? But I was quite fortunate 'cause I believed in what Alex believed in. No' because o' Alex, because a' my family's mining, an' I wholeheartedly believed in it.

I was changed – through bitterness. That's the reason I was changed, definitely bitter. I don't blame the unions one bit, they tried everything for us. I blame the government, the Tory government. Because they had the ba' at their foot, they could've reinstated oor men, put oor minds at rest, but it just didnae seem to work that way. But I was very bitter. Even bitter to the fact that even when the police came to the door one night aboot my son, he had broken a window, I wouldn't even bring them in or nothing because I hated them, I still dae.

A' I hope is I never ever need them because I'll never, ever be the same wi' them. The miners wernae perfect, I'm no' saying that, but what they did to them was a total disgrace. I would never have believed it. I used to say to Alex 'Aw come off it, youse are daein something,' but that day just finished me, down in London.

It was a big rally and I'll never forget it. The treatment they gave they men. Certainly, don't get me wrong, the miners retaliated at the last, but provoked definitely.

There's one area of work in Fallin, which is a florist's that pays them £2 or £1.80 an hour, which is a disgrace. But my son and that, there's nothing for them. He'd to go away outside the place tae get a job.

I've heard people going on aboot Scargill, even miners. How wrong they are, because tae me there wasnae a better man suited to lead them. A very educated man. And when he came up here I used to go just to hear him and I thought he was brilliant. Even the likes a' John McCormack, John is really good tae. Quite a few o' them could be persuaded because o' their men, but I wouldnae need Alex tae tell me anything because I knew wi' a' my family being miners what everything was like. I don't begrudge a minute of the year that the pit was oot on strike, I grudged after it what they done to him, no' reinstating him. They made him oot as though he was some sort o' an animal.

I'll never forgive them to my dying day for it, never. And that's how even the noo wi' the Timex dispute, it brings back all the memories. What they can dae to the people, they can walk o'er the people. If people don't take a stance and stand up the unions will be finished.

There's insecurity now wi' Alex's job. There's definitely going to be pay-offs. So we're expecting Alex to be paid off. But then that's just something we'll need to live wi', that's what life's all about. You've just to take the bad wi' the good. Too many people noo just cannae take the pressure. Hopefully he'll no' be paid off but we'll master that when the time comes.

INDEX